G000122364

Characters of the
Spanish Civil War
and Other Stories

Julio A. Gonzalo

Foreword by John Beaumont

Ciencia y Cultura

Madrid 2014

Characters of the Spanish Civil War

1st Edition June 2014

© Julio A. Gonzalo

© Asociación Española Ciencia y Cultura
c/ Pavía 4, 1º D. 28013 Madrid (España)
Fax: (34) 91-4978579
www.cienciaycultura.com
E-mail: julio.gonzalo@uam.es
E-mail : aecienciaycultura@gmail.com

ISBN: 978-84-942740-0-8
ISBN eBook: 978-84-942740-1-5

FOREWORD

In my country of Great Britain the overwhelming majority of writers on the Spanish Civil War have taken the Republican side. A major exception early on was that doughty Catholic apologist, Arnold Lunn (see *Spanish Rehearsal* [1937]). Another was the poet Roy Campbell (see *Flowering Rifles: A Poem from the Battlefield of Spain* [1936]). Both writers were very much in a minority. And so it has remained. Of course, this approach of taking a morally tolerant line in respect of the Left has not been confined to Spain. Even now *Uncle* Joe Stalin and Mao-Tse-Tung tend to get off relatively lightly when compared to the Fascist leaders. Of course, when it comes to Hitler, it's all relative, since all three were responsible for millions of deaths and it is very artificial to assess them by an exact mathematical calculation (though even there the figures of those murdered by the Communists are recognized now to have been considerably higher).

When it comes to General Franco in Spain (and also, of course, to Antonio Salazar in Portugal), there are relevant and important distinctions to be made. As Professor Gonzalo points out in the introduction to this book, much disinformation was peddled, primarily by the Soviet Union, about General Franco, and this has often been accepted completely uncritically by my countrymen (and writers in several other countries) in their works on Spain. It is something like the way that Senator Joseph McCarthy in the United States has been treated as something of a monster (and *McCarthyism* as almost the epitome of all evil). In the case of McCarthy, the opening up of the documentary records following the fall of the Soviet Union should have changed all that, but there has been a distinct lack of acceptance, on the part of the so-called scholars (the American writer M. Stanton Evans being excluded from this charge), of the truth that was revealed. There has been a similar approach in the case of General Franco.

In addition, although again there has been a lack of appreciation of this, there is in any case a much more positive aspect to the life and work of General Franco than has usually been set out in the majority of published works. For instance, as Professor Gonzalo points out, there is the economic prosperity in the later days of Franco's rule, and in addition the important, and often forgotten fact, that the Spanish people voted freely *Yes* to Franco in the 1966 referendum.

However, there is something much more important for which Franco deserves to go down in history with a favorable review, and it is something that is also brought out well in this book. This is that the positive consequences of the Nationalist victory in the Spanish Civil War were crucial for the future history of Europe after the Second World War. The truth is that if Spain had been Communist at that time, bearing in mind that the Soviets had swallowed up half of Europe, that Germany was shattered, and that Communism was strong in France and Italy, then there would have been a distinct possibility that the Soviet Union would have taken over the whole of Europe.

There is, then, a need for what might be called *another view* of the Spanish Civil War emphasizing the valuable role of Franco and that of the many brave representatives of the Nationalist force during that war. Professor Gonzalo has provided this by his examination of some of the most fascinating characters involved in that epoch-making struggle.

All readers will be moved by the stories contained in these chapters. We see acts of great heroism and also on a smaller scale much that is characteristic of courageous behavior under conditions of great stress to the individuals concerned. It would be invidious to pick out particular chapters, but I was particularly moved by the chapter entitled «Hispania Martir», an account of martyrdom during the war. What terrible deeds were done in those times. The author also brings out the drama of the epic siege of the Alcazar of Toledo. Then there is the detailed account of the progression of thought of Garcia Morente leading to his conversion, particularly fascinating to me in view of my work on converts (as is, of course, the chapter on Ambassador Hayes, another convert to the Catholic faith). Memorable also, and instructive, is the vibrant account of the confrontation at the University of Salamanca between Miguel de Unamuno and Millán Astray. Finally, all stories, even of war, have their lighter moments. Be sure, then, dear reader, to examine with care the chapter on Franco and President Eisenhower, and in particular the joke, about Napoleon and the relationship between generals and colonels, told to Franco by Eisenhower's aide, Vernon Walters.

Professor Gonzalo divides his book into two sections. The first deals with the Civil War itself. The second reviews certain events leading on from the war and their effect on the post-war situation. In respect of the former, he is surely correct when he states that although the Spanish Civil War was both a war involving a struggle in relation to liberation and secession, it was in a more major sense a war of religion. Great numbers of Catholic priests, nuns, and laymen were slaughtered, and, of course, this *purge* began well before the actual beginning of the war itself. In addition, many hundreds of churches were destroyed and the whole framework of the Church's religious practice attacked. The significance of this cannot be overstated. These facts must be kept in mind whilst reading the main text if only to appreciate in a more objective fashion the great significance of the events themselves.

The author has done us a very useful service in redressing the unbalanced nature of many of the earlier authorities on this subject. His book is of great importance and deserves a wide audience.

John Beaumont
Feast of Saint John of God
8th March 2014

PROLOGUE

As Ion Mihai and Ronald J. Rychlak have shown (*Disinformation: Former Spy Chief Reveals Secret Strategies for Undermining Freedom, Attacking Religion, and Promoting Terrorism*, WND Books, June 2013), «the absolutely worst –and often irreparable– damage done to the free world was caused by the Kremlin's operations that were designed to *change the past*» (emphasis mine).

Dezinformatsiya constituted a very highly classified *disinformation* specialty used intensively by the Soviet Union since the time of Stalin. The Kremlin was engaged in the framing of Pope Pius XII since 1945, of General Franco since 1975, and, perhaps, more indirectly, of President Reagan since 2008. And of many others, of course.

Aleksandr Solzhenitsyn said it well in a few words: «In our country, the lie has become not just a moral category but a pillar of the State».

Alojzije Cardinal Stepinac of Croatia, József Cardinal Mindszenty of Hungary, Josef Cardinal Beran of Czechoslovakia, and Stefan Cardinal Wyszynski of Poland were *framed* as Nazi collaborators, and persecuted, starved or beaten by means of evidence from fabricated documents in the post-war years.

The play *Der Stellvertreter: Ein christliches Trauerspiel* (*The Deputy: A Christian Tragedy*) by Rolf Hochhuth, which portrayed Pius XII in the late fifties and early sixties as Hitler's

Pope triggered the framing of that Pope. At the beginning, Pius XII's reputation, as a protagonist of the resistance against the Nazis (highly praised by Churchill, Roosevelt, Adenauer, Einstein, and even Golda Meir) was not affected. But years later, when new generations, ignorant of the true nature of Soviet Communism, were coming to maturity, the KGB-infused *disinformation* in Europe and America about the role of Pius XII in the years of Nazi power became increasingly successful.

The case with Franco is more complicated. During the Civil War, the Spanish leader was portrayed as a lackey of Hitler and Mussolini. Later, after he resisted successfully Hitler's attempt to cross the Peninsula and take Gibraltar, closing the Mediterranean from the West, and sending later the Blue Division to the East to placate the Nazi leader, Franco was often portrayed as a sheer opportunist. And still later, when in the sixties and early seventies a mixture of liberal (Navarro Rubio, Ullastres) and authoritarian (Girón, Solís) policies brought unprecedented economic prosperity to the country, his image changed to that of a benevolent dictator, respected by most Western leaders (Churchill, De Gaulle, Adenauer, Eisenhower...). That certainly was his image abroad in his last decade as Chief of State. And it must not be forgotten that in the Referendum of 1966 (Franco: *Yes* or *No*; Continuity: *Yes* or *No*), all foreign observers agreed that the large majority of the Spanish people voted freely *Yes* to Franco.

Who could have imagined in 1975 that about forty years later «the past would have changed» to such an extent that the previous image of Franco's Spain would be reversed, erasing completely from the public consciousness, not only the clear victory, but also the long years of peace and prosperity?

* * *

It was October 1990, in Madrid. I had managed to organize a Symposium on *Physics and Religion in Perspective* with the generous cooperation of Banco Bilbao-Vizcaya thanks to my good friend Professor Pedro Echenique (University of the Basque Country, San Sebastián), graciously complemented by UNED (*Universidad Nacional de Educación a Distancia*). The event was to take place at the magnificent Lecture Room of the RSEM (*Real Sociedad Económica Matritense*) located at the Torre de los Lujanes.

The Program included lectures by Stanley L. Jaki (*Physics and the Universe: From the Sumerians to the End of the 20th Century*); Sánchez del Río (*The Centuries of Copernicus, Kepler and Galileo*); Jerzy A. Janik (*Philosophical Problems Resulting from New Aspects of the Physics of Chaos*); Julio A. Gonzalo (*Cosmology and Transcendence*) and Mariano Artigas *(E. Mach and P. Duhem: The Philosophical Meaning of the History of Science*).

The night before the opening session of the Symposium I had invited to dinner in *Zarauz*, a restaurant near Plaza de la Ópera, to Professor Jaki, scheduled to give the opening lecture the following morning, and to Professor Janik, another of the speakers, a distinguished physicist from the University of Cracow, who was a close personal friend of Pope John Paul II from the time Karl Wojtila was Archbishop of Cracow. Professor Jaki, an Hungarian born American with a strong personality, had been made (or was soon to be made) a member of the Pontifical Academia of Sciences by the Polish Pope. And Professor Janik, who was in Madrid with his wife to participate in another meeting on the Physics of Chaos, was certainly a Polish gentleman and a well known scholar of international reputation.

At some point in the after-dinner conversation Professor Janik asked me, very politely, a potentially conflictive question:

- Professor Gonzalo, let me ask you the following. After so many years of authoritarian government in Spain, how do you think the young generation of Spaniards is doing with regard to the exercise of their personal freedom?

- Well –I began to say– , I think it would be incorrect to make a parallel between the situation in Spain and the situation in Central or Eastern Europe under Communist rule...

- Look –interrupted Professor Jaki–, in history, there are crucial moments, decisive moments, at which events take place which have later incalculable consequences difficult to anticipate. That was the case with the Spanish rising against the Republican government in 1936, when Spain was being pushed into the hands of Soviet Russia... At the time that General

10

Franco, in civilian clothes, picked up the *Dragon Rapide* to fly from the Canary Islands to Tetouan (Spanish Morocco) to take command of the Spanish African Army, few could have imagined the immediate consequences, and nobody could have foreseen the very far reaching consequences of the Nationalist victory in Spain. After the Second World War the Soviets had taken over half Europe, Germany was completely broken, and the Communist parties in France and Italy were very strong... A Communist Spain at that time would have meant the take over of the entire continent by the Soviets. Fortunately, after some hesitation at the beginning, the U.S. reacted and arrived at an agreement with the Spanish government. Spain was, and is still, of course, very strategically located as the Western gate to the Mediterranean, and she was then the only firm anti-communist country in western Europe, at a time when Britain was not quite fully recovered from the war.

Professor Janik was listening attentively, and I was somewhat surprised that a scholar of the calibre of Professor Jaki had such a clear perception of how much, there and then, was involved at the time for Spain, and, in the near future, for Europe and the World, when General Franco arrived at Tetouan to lead the Spanish African Army under very precarious, almost desperate conditions. Later, I had long talks with Professor Jaki, a Benedictine monk from Pannonhalma Abbey transplanted to Princeton who had good reasons, personal reasons to know... I had lived from 1962 to 1976 in the American Continent, and had had numerous discussions about the significance of the Spanish Civil War with many colleagues from all over the world (American, Japanese, Chinese, Russian, German, British, French, Italian...). Later on, back in Spain, I had also conversations with foreign visitors of all persuasions. Most people, even generally well informed people, have, in my opinion, a very incomplete and distorted idea of what was really at the stake in the Spanish Civil War. It is well known that more books have been written on the Spanish Civil War (which was not, it should be noted, a mere prelude of the Second World War) than on the Second World War itself. Foreign involvement with both sides during the Civil War was important but not decisive in its final outcome. This balanced, more or less, each

11

other. But those who helped the defeated Republicans came out victorious in 1945, while those who helped the Nationalists (among other things, the Nationalists had to seek Italian and German support because there was no one else to provide military support) came out defeated. It is quite wrong therefore to identify the Spanish Nationalists with the Nazis.

The Spanish Civil War was several wars in one: a *war of liberation* (from the imminent menace of Soviet oppression), a *war of secession* (against the Basque and Catalan separatisms), but, above all, a *war of religion*, with hundreds of Catholic churches burned, and many priests, nuns and laymen killed, *even before* the beginning of the war, in 1934 and from February to July of 1936.

I hope the short stories collected in this book help to illustrate that triple character of the Spanish Civil War.

* * *

I am truly grateful to John Beaumont for his painstaking correction of my poor English and for his wise observations.

J.A.G.

THE CIVIL WAR

Calvo Sotelo

Franco

The Alcazar of Toledo

Unamuno and Millán Astray

Hispania Martir

Captain Cortés, defender
of Santa María de la Cabeza

Decorated Cities

Cardinal Gomá and the Bishops' Collective Letter

García Lorca and Muñoz Seca

Testament of José Antonio Primo de Rivera

García Morente's *Extraordinary Event*

Azaña

José Díaz and *El Campesino*

Prieto and Largo Caballero

Mola

Varela and Yagüe

Félix Schlayer and *Pasionaria*

CALVO SOTELO

José Calvo Sotelo was born in Tuy (Pontevedra) in 1893. He was chosen as Minister of Government and Finance by Don Miguel Primo de Rivera when at a period of great unrest he proclaimed the Dictatorship (1925), with king Alfonso XIII's approval, after years of social violence. Calvo Sotelo was considered at the time a competent and successful Finance Minister. When the 2nd Republic was proclaimed in Spain, Calvo Sotelo moved to France. Later, he was elected member of the Spanish Parliament (*Las Cortes*) and came back as leader of the Monarchist Minority in 1933. Re-elected in February 1936, he was one of the most outspoken critics of the weak Republican Government, a very outspoken spectator of the rapid deterioration of law and order. He was assassinated in Madrid on the 13th July 1936.

On 4th February 1936, days before the general elections, to be held on the 16th, a National Counterrevolutionary Front was reluctantly formed to oppose the Popular Front dominated by the extreme Left. The National Front included Gil-Robles (CEDA, Spanish Confederation of Autonomous Right), Calvo Sotelo (Monarchists) and the Traditionalists (Carlists). On 16th February, even before the final recount of the votes had been completed, the Popular Front lost no time to proclaim victory. After the final recount it was clear that the Popular Front had obtained a relative majority, but not an absolute one. However, when the new Parliament convened, the Popular Front questioned several of the seats initially won by the Right and managed to convert an incomplete and partial victory into an overwhelming one.

Public order deteriorated very rapidly and the number of churches burnt by socialists, communists and anarchists, as well as the number of victims of shooting squads from both sides grew rapidly.

Casares Quiroga, another man from Galicia, the region in which Calvo Sotelo was born, had formed a Government with cabinet members drawn mainly from Azaña's Left Republican Party. He said at the time that he needed no support from the Popular Front to govern.

On 29th May Calvo Sotelo made a dramatic speech at the Cortes:

> Parliament is haughtily, pompously, presiding over the Spanish anarchy: the legislative power tries to give an impression of normality , while all the other powers, the whole of Spanish life, are the personification of chaos, disorder and abnormality... You are living on anarchy... because to repress it you would have to forfeit the political oxygen which these extreme forces give you. Have the courage to die slaying anarchy and Spain will be saved!
> (See W. Carroll, *The Last Crusade*, 1996)

Early in July, a Falangist hit squad had shot and killed José Castillo, the Communist Lieutenant of the Assault Guard (a new police body created by the Republic, a body which was then generally considered them left leaning). Castillo had shot some Falangists in a violent battle at Madrid's Cemetery on 17th April.

On 13th July, at two o'clock in the morning, a group led by Lieutenant Condés, a close friend of Castillo, obtained authorization from the Minister of the Interior to arrest some Falangists. They went first to the house of Antonio Goicoechea, a friend and political colleague of Calvo Sotelo, and did not find him. Then they went to the home of Gil-Robles, and did not find him there either. Finally they went to Calvo Sotelo's home and found him there.

Calvo Sotelo's life had been threatened at the Cortes by Marguerite Nelken (on 7th May) and Valentín Galarza (on 1st July), both socialist representatives. At the great debate in the Cortes (16th June) on the general collapse of law and order, Calvo Sotelo said in response to the threats to his life :

I recall the answer given by St. Dominic of Silos to a Spanish king: «Sire, my life you may take from me, but more you cannot take». Is it not indeed, better to perish gloriously, than to live in contempt?

Dolores Ibárruri, *La Pasionaria*, communist representative at the Cortes, was rumored to had said to him: «This is your last speech». Hugh Thomas has been unable to document Dolores Ibárruri's saying those words to Calvo Sotelo then and there. Félix Schlayer, consul of Norway in Madrid 1936-37, on the other hand recounts Dolores Ibárruri's words to him in November 1936:

At the end of the conversation I asked *La Pasionaria* how did she imagine that the two halves of Spain, separated from one another by such an abysmal hate could live together as a single people and support each other (after that blood confrontation). She then exploded saying: «Impossible! That is impossible! There is no other solution than one half exterminating the other half!».

Informed that the authority in charge had given instructions to his escorts not to protect him in case of an attempted of assassination, Calvo Sotelo had remarked that perhaps his murder would give the organizer of the Nationalist rising the occasion to unite and act while there was still time.

At three o'clock in the morning of 13th July, fatal knocks on the door of Calvo Sotelo's home announced Condés and his Assault Guards. Calvo Sotelo told his wife that he would let them take him to the police headquarters and that he would phone her from there... «unless these gentlemen are going to blow out my brains».

Victoriano Cuenca, a young Galician Socialist accompanying Condés, did precisely that when the police truck driven along Velázquez street crossed Ayala street. The truck proceeded then to the cemetery dumping Calvo Sotelo's body inside without identification.

On Tuesday 14th, the funeral for the eternal rest of Calvo Sotelo was held at Madrid's cemetery. His mortal remains, at his request, were wearing a Franciscan habit. His friend Goicoechea spoke then and there:

Before that flag placed like a cross on your chest, before God that hears and sees us, we make a solemn oath to put our lives to this triple objective: to imitate your example, to avenge your death, and to save Spain, which is all one thing. To save Spain will be to avenge your death and to imitate your example will be the sure way to save Spain.

Gil-Robles said wryly: «Calvo Sotelo's blood will drown the Government». After Calvo Sotelo's funeral, a battle between Falangists and Assault Guards resulted in four deaths. Prieto, who had been for some time warning about the coming disaster, was eloquent:

If the reaction dreams of a bloodless *coup d'état* like the one in 1923, it is entirely mistaken. If it thinks that it will find the regime defenseless, it is deluding itself. To conquer it will have to surmount the human barrier with which the proletarian masses bar its way. There will be –I have said it many times– a battle to death, because each side knows that the adversary, if he wins, will give him no quarter. Even if this were the way it had to be, a decisive engagement would be better than this acrimonious blood-letting.

FRANCO

My father, who, at 24 already married and father of three sons, fought in 1936-39 the Civil War (with many others of his generation) in the Nationalist Army, had in his personal library a copy of *Franco* by Joaquín Arrarás (6th edition), 1938, printed in Imprenta Aldecoa, Burgos.

That book had already in 1938 the following editions abroad:
In Argentina, by Editorial Poblet of Buenos Aires.
In Italy, under the title *Il Generalissimo Franco*, by Editorial, Bompiani, Milan. Introduction by Farinacci, translation by Cesare Giardini.

In France, under the title *Le Général Franco*, by Éditions de la France. Translation of Jeanne Sabatier and Louis Blanc.

In Chile, under the title *Franco, Cuarto Caudillo de la Época*, by Editorial Zig-Zag.

In New York, under the title *Francisco Franco*, by The Bruce Publishing Company, Milwaukee (*sic*), Viss (*sic*). Translator, Antonio Espinosa.

In Germany, by the Hoffmann und Campe Verlag, Berlin-Hamburg.

Below this list of foreign editions, Arrarás informs his readers that new editions were just coming out in London, Copenhagen, Havana, Prague, The Hague and other capitals.

In the Prologue I mentioned Fr. Jaki in connection with Franco's flight to Tetouan. I don't know if he had read Arrarás' book or not, but it is worthwhile to summarize here the chapter entitled «De Tenerife a Tetuán», which recounts the story with vivid drama:

> Soon after arriving at Santa Cruz de Tenerife, Franco finds himself prisoner of the Popular Front [...]. He is watched day and night; his mail is intercepted; his telephone intercepted...
>
> - An attempt against your life is underway he is told.
> - Two years ago –responds Franco– Moscow has sentenced me to death.
>
> Around Command Headquarters roam strange people locating themselves at strategic points. The Civil Guard has news of the plot... The government knows about it and, being the guarantees scarce, the garrison's officers, at the request of the Senior Colonel, agree to organize a permanent personal guard. Franco is not aware... Even the changes in time schedules are made without his knowledge when his presence at an official event is arranged.
>
> An attempt on his life in La Laguna is aborted. Another in the Villa of Orotava is frustrated also [...] the last criminal attempt takes place on 13th July [...]. The assailants (three) attempt to climb the garden wall to enter the central pavilion where the private rooms of Franco were located [...]. When they appeared above the wall, one of the watching sentinels shouts and fires. The guard outside fires also, but the assailants escape...
>
> The wife and daughter of the general were also guarded by a service of surveillance.
>
> On 14th July there arrives at Santa Cruz de Tenerife the diplomat don Juan Antonio de Sangróniz to inform the general of the latest

news [...]. The airplane that must take Franco to Tetouan should arrive at Las Palmas the following day.

The following night General Franco talks extensively with close friends on the events to come...

- Things seem to be ready [...]. And we cannot wait much longer because the advances of anarchy are so considerable that very soon the possibilities of a reaction will be zero...

- In one week –comments one of the present– everything will be favorably solved...

- If the military coup is successful, yes; but the government has at its disposal many resources [...]. If the coup fails, the war will be bloody and long: the enemies of Spain are powerful and many [...] I have absolute faith in victory. I am convinced that Spain, after a difficult period, [...] will recover soon.

In the morning of the 16th unexpected news arrived by phone to Tenerife; news as sad as unexpected.

General don Amadeo Balmes, Military Commander of Las Palmas, had died when his pistol shot itself accidentally [...]. The general had been for days testing fire arms so that «the boys had at their disposal useful fire arms and not cheap rubbish».

Franco phoned the Ministry of War to inform them that he had the intention to go to Las Palmas in order to preside at the burial.

- They may take the opportunity to dismiss me...

The dismissal did not materialize. The War Undersecretary, on behalf of the Minister, authorized him. At twelve thirty that night, General Franco with his wife and daughter embarked in the inter-island ship Viera y Clavijo. His aides, four escort officers, and the juridical prosecutor Mr. Martínez Fusset came with him.

At the waterfront were all the garrison's officers and many civilians. The general was carrying as his only baggage a little suitcase which contained a black suit.

Colonel González Peral was the last to give him his farewell:

- May God be with you, my General.

- I hope so.

Once General Balmes' burial was over [...] at noon time, on the 17th, Franco devoted all his time to receive contacts at his hotel, from which he did not get out.

At three in the morning the escort officers were awakened by Mr. Martínez Fusset bringing sensational news:

- The African troops have risen. Be extremely cautious.

Soon thereafter Franco, who already knew it, having been informed at two fifteen by Tenerife's Commandant, showed up.

He was in civilian clothes and with a suitcase in his hands. He entered the car awaiting him and went to the Command. At that moment General Orgaz arrived. He would take over the Civil Government the following morning [...]. Franco wrote down a manifesto and gave the first orders [...]. He stayed at the Command till eleven, at which time he left to pick up the plane...

The car took him to the waterfront where the carrier was waiting to bring him to the Gando airfield. Franco hesitates, he wants to say good bye to his wife and daughter, but he quickly resolves: «Tell them that I left to do something but will be back soon», he orders to his officers.

Franco is wearing a black suit and is well shaved, without his characteristic moustache. He wears spectacles and has a diplomatic passport in his pocket.

At Gando airport there is a mysterious twin-engine plane, the O.H. Rapide, a six seater, from Croydon, with British tourists: Major Hugo B.C. Pollard, expert in firearms from Scotland Yard, his daughter Diana and her friend Dorothy Watson. How have they arrived at Las Palmas?

Once agreed upon that Franco would go to Tetouan by plane, don Francisco Herrera Oria had been put in charge to rent a rapid plane. Soon he got the money and he contacted, in order to make the arrangements, don Luis A. Bolin, a journalist resident in London, who signed the contract with Olley Air Company, and invited his friend Mr. Pollard to make the plane trip to Las Palmas, to avoid any suspicions, as a tourist accompanied by his daughter and another young lady to avoid any suspicion. Captain Beeb, an expert pilot, would fly the plane.

- Would you commit yourself to fly to the Canary Islands on condition of not landing, under any pretext, in Spanish territory? – asked Bolin–. Once in Las Palmas you must pick up a certain person to take him to Tetouan.

Captain Beeb accepted.

He left Croydon (London) on the 11th. He stopped at Bordeaux and Porto. Another stop came at Casablanca where Bolin would be waiting for him on his way back. And, finally, Las Palmas. There, the pilot, a mechanic and the British passengers, unaware of what awaited them, would stay surprised and confused.

The following day Captain Beeb heard a discrete knock on his door and responded: «Come in». An unknown visitor asked him a battery of questions. At the end, confidentially, he told him:

- The general wishes to see you.
- What general?

Then the visitor as him to be silent and said:
- Do you know where the church is?
- I know where the cathedral is…
- At four o'clock you must be there at the main gate. A car will stop in front of you and the driver will make a signal. Come in and he will take you to the mountain.

«A little later –says Captain Bebb–, they introduced me to General Orgaz who questioned me again». The general said goodbye and another Spaniard insinuated that he must forget everything. «We will see how all this ends up…», thought the captain.

Towards four o'clock, a new messenger showed up. He spoke impeccable English. After exchanging greetings, he invited me to accompany him to the terrace outside… At last, the enigma is going to be uncovered. But, at the last minute, there is a counter-order. He was to come up to the mountain and stay there under cover till the mysterious passenger is ready for the trip.

The following day things begin to clear up. The Spanish visitor of the previous day comes looking for him at four o'clock in the morning […]. He follows the visitor to another room and they wait. At twelve o'clock, he receives a second command: Get out!

Escorted by a Patrol of armed motorists, he is driven to the airport […] at last he sees the plane in the middle of the field ready to go.
- Are the tanks filled?
- Everything is ready –replies the mechanic.
- And the passenger?
- Look at him.

On the nearby beach a boat brings a few passengers. One of them approaches the pilot and says:
- I am General Franco.

The motor begins to run. The general says farewell one by one to those who accompany him. Into the plane come then the military aviator Villalobos and Franco Salgado, his cousin.

It was exactly 2.10 pm the 18th July 1936.

A brief stop in Agadir, and forward, to Casablanca, where the airplane lands at 9.30 pm. There was Bolin […]. They move to a small hotel nearby, where, after dinner they talk about Spain till long into the night. At four in the morning, without any sleep, they depart for the airport. In half an hour they are flying again […]. They cross the sky under a radiant blue sky. At seven in the morning… Tetouan!

On the airfield, a large crowd. The plane flies low, and Franco recognizes some familiar faces.

Then, the landing. With the motor still running, cheers and applauses. Franco appears smiling. Lieutenant Colonel Yagüe salutes him after the landing and legionary forces in formation make him honors.

At night, Franco's voice is broadcasted to all Spain, through the miracle of radio waves:

- After taking Command in Tetouan [...] I send my most enthusiastic salute to all garrisons loyal to our Fatherland. Spain has saved herself. You can be proud of being Spaniards [...]. Have blind faith. Don't ever hesitate [...]- Our movement is sweeping forward. There is no human force capable of stopping it [...]. Long life to Spain!

The rising, as a matter of fact, had failed in most big cities, Madrid, Barcelona, Valencia... Only Zaragoza, Seville, Corunna were for the rebels. In the first few months of the war, Franco was still hopeful of a quick victory, but it soon became evident that it would be necessarily a long and bloody war.

Paul Johnson (*Modern Times: The World from the Twenties to the Nineties*, New York, 1992, pp. 330-331), a relatively unsympathetic British historian, says it well:

The Nationalists won primarily because of the capacity and judgement of Franco. Though Franco was an unlovable man [...] he must be accounted one of the most successful public men of the century. His cold heart went with a cool head, great intelligence and formidable reserves of courage and will... Franco thought war a hateful business, from which gross cruelty was inseparable; it might sometimes be necessary to advance civilization. He was in the tradition of the Romans, the crusaders, the conquistadors, the *tercios* of Parma...Franco was never a fascist or had the smallest belief in any kind of Utopia or system.

THE ALCAZAR OF TOLEDO

During the Spanish Civil War, the siege of the Alcazar of Toledo was one such epic event which amazed and held captive world opinion during two months. It was by no means the only epic event. There were others, but the Alcazar's heroic and incredible resistance against all odds was unique in that it had a happy end (see e.g. Ángel Palomimo, *Defensa del Alcázar: Una Epopeya de Nuestro Tiempo*, Planeta, Barcelona, 1985; Cecil Elby, *The Siege of the Alcazar*, New York, 1965; Warren Carroll, *The Last Crusade*, Christendom Press, Front Royal, Virginia, 1996). We summarize below the vivid account of Warren Carroll.

The Alcazar is located in a gigantic rock dominating the Tagus river as it passes through Toledo in the middle of the New Castilian plain. It was built by Emperor Charles V in the sixteenth century, and it had later become a military academy rebuilt after a fire in 1887, with an exceptionally strong framework of steel girders and walls up to twelve feet high. Four impressive towers crowned by spires stood at the four corners of the heavily built building. The *Picadero*, used as a riding academy, was adjoining the Alcazar on the east side and the Santiago barracks for troops assigned permanently to the

Academy were just below, overlooking the Tagus river a hundred feet below. The Government building housed the offices of the military governor of Toledo and his staff.

Ángel Palomino notes that the history of Spain registers several conflicts in which a handful of Spaniards encircled by an enemy overwhelmingly superior in numbers and means, decides to resist at all costs to the last man. In those cases the proverbial fighting virtues of Spaniards, sobriety, superhuman capacity to stand suffering, unspeakable endurance, have astonished friends and foes all around. Numancia and Sagunto in classical antiquity; Zamora and Tarifa during the Spanish Reconquest; Cadiz, Gerona and Saragossa during the War of Independence against Napoleon. Baler, in the Philippines, when the last handful of the Spanish soldiers refused to acknowledge defeat before the overwhelming superiority of the American forces.

In the Spanish Civil War the defenders of the Alcazar of Toledo did literally astonish the whole world with their heroic defense under utterly desperate conditions.

Till the Alcazar was liberated, most journalists from all over the world granted the rebels little chances of succeeding. When the almost exhausted Legionaries and the vanguard Moroccan troops arrived to rescue the surviving defenders of the Alcazar, those astonished journalists were the first to recognize that the rising might succeed against all odds.

The numerous academy riding horses were kept in stables at the basement. From the Government building, a steep winding road called the Zig Zag led up to the north terrace of the Alcazar building, which was closed off by an iron gate. Facing the Government building, there was a narrow street leading to the main square, the Plaza de Zocodover.

No cadets were at the Academy in July 1936 because it was summer vacation. Colonel José Moscardó was the Academy commandant. He was sixty years old, six feet tall, heavy built and passionately loyal to Church and country. He had graduated from the Academy forty years before. On the morning of 18th July, he heard the radio reports by the Spanish government informing the population of the *doomed* rising of the African army in Morocco. He decided on the spot to drive to Madrid to consult with trusted army officers stationed there. Some of them knew what had been planned and told him. He had met Franco only once, but he decided to join the rising immediately. The arms factory in Toledo could be of great value for the rebels. Colonel Moscardó hurried back Toledo to take the city for the rebels or, at least, to prevent the forces of the Republican Army from taking it over. That evening, he assembled a large group of officers in the Alcazar and, as the highest ranking officer, he succeeded in gaining their support for the rising. Colonel Romero, chief of the Civil Guard of Toledo, persuaded him, wisely, to delay a public announcement until substantial forces of the Civil Guard and a large supply of ammunition from the arms factory were already inside the Alcazar. A clash between armed workers and Civil Guardsmen the night before in Plaza de Zocodover had already taken place. And civilians seeking protection from the revolutionaries were already coming in.

On Sunday 19th, early in the morning, Mass was offered in the Alcazar chapel. In the front rank of worshipers Colonel Moscardó knelt. There would pass fifty four days «of fire and blood» before another Mass, this time said by Canon Camarasa (as recounted below in more detail), was held in the Alcazar of Toledo. Later that Sunday the War Ministry called Moscardó from Madrid ordering him to turn over the arms kept in the Alcazar. Moscardó demanded the order in writing. The War Ministry official promised to send the written order by next morning. Toledo was quiet that night.

During Monday, 20th July, the same day the rebels in the *Cuartel de la Montaña* in Madrid were massacred by the armed revolutionaries, a stream of Civil Guardsmen, many with their wives and children, were coming quietly to the Alcazar, some in cars or trucks, some in horses or mules, totaling over 600. Twenty three Civil Guardsmen who had been captured on their way to the Alcazar were either shot on the spot or sent to Madrid to be executed. Moscardó called a meeting with all the officers in the evening and said, in no uncertain terms, that the time for decision had come. All present committed themselves to the rising, many bringing their families with them. Not so Moscardó. The following day in the morning they totaled about 1800. There were approximately 700 Civil Guardsmen, 250 Army officers and Academy staff, about 100 men of military age, Falangists, traditionalists, members of Catholic Actions or other Church associations, 550 women and 200 children.

Apparently, in spite of the bad news about the rising in Madrid, Barcelona and Valencia, most of them were confident that soon the rising would prevail and that they would be rescued.

A proclamation stating that Toledo no longer accepted the authority of Madrid's Government was read at seven o'clock in the morning, first in the courtyard of the Alcazar, besides the statue of Charles V, and then in the Plaza de Zocodover. A government airplane circled the Alcazar later in the morning, dropping leaflets urging the garrison to desert the officers. Not one man left.

That afternoon the roar of motors and a heavy dust cloud announced the arrival of cars and trucks carrying 3000 men (mostly militia) from Madrid, commanded by General José Riquelme, the highest ranking officer supporting the revolutionary Republic. Machine gun fire from the defenders of the Alcazar quickly stopped the advance. An armored car sent forward by the attackers was blown up by a grenade. The demand of General Riquelme that the Alcazar surrender in fifteen minutes was ignored. In the midst of this attack, Moscardó managed to bring eight out of ten trucks loaded with ammunition from the arms factory to the Alcazar, enough for his men to fight for many weeks.

When Riquelme telephoned Moscardó that evening to demand his surrender, Moscardó refused, and being asked why, he replied:

> Because I love Spain and I have confidence in General Franco. Furthermore –he added– it would be dishonorable to surrender the arms of gentlemen to your Red rabble.

The next day, Wednesday 22nd, Riquelme's men shot and shelled the Alcazar with little effect, but Moscardó was forced to withdraw all his men from the city, bringing them into the sheltering walls of the Alcazar. At a meeting with his officers, in a room lit by acetylene torches, because electricity had been cut off, Moscardó explained that the rebels plan was that Mola's forces would march South, while Franco's forces would march

North, relieving them on their way to Madrid. They had plenty of ammunition. Three cisterns and a swimming pool provided sufficient drinking water. And Moscardó believed that food could be obtained by raids into the city. In the middle of the meeting, Francisco Barnés, Giral's Minister of Education, called Moscardó to urge his surrender. Moscardó asked the officers present to vote. The majority voted to maintain their resistance and he informed Barnés.

Then you will be responsible for the destruction of the Alzacar – said Barnés–. I can only do my duty to Spain, sir –replied Moscardó–. We have the means to annihilate you. This is the last time you have the opportunity to avoid spilling blood. Colonel, if you do not change your mind, I must order the attack immediately – said Barnés–. We are ready to receive it –replied Moscardó.

The Thursday 23rd, at seven o'clock in the morning, Moscardo's 24-year-old son Luis was picked up for questioning by a military patrol. The head of Toledo's *checa* (revolutionary committees organized to question and torture persons suspected of disloyalty to the Republic), a lawyer named Cándido Cabello, knew Luis Moscardó by sight and decided on the spot to use him to surrender the Alcazar. It was ten o'clock in the morning. After identifying himself, Cabello said to Colonel Moscardó:

You are responsible for all the crimes and everything else happening in Toledo. I give you ten minutes to surrender the Alcazar. If you don't, I'll shoot your son Luis who is standing here beside me.

I believe you – said Moscardó.

To show you that what I am saying is the truth –said Caballero–he will speak to you.

Papa! –cried Luis at the phone.

What is it, my boy?

Nothing. They say they will shoot me if the Alcazar does not surrender. But don't worry about me.

If it is true, commend your soul to God, shout «Viva España!» and die like a hero. Good-bye, my son, a kiss.

Good-bye, father… a very strong kiss.

Then, when Cabello was again at the phone, Moscardo said: The Alcazar will never surrender! You might as well forget about the period of grace…

Cabello slammed down the phone receiver and cursed violently. Moscardó stood silent for some moments and without saying anything to those around him, walked out into his room and closed the door. His son was not killed immediately, but was shot one month later, with the Alcazar still under siege.

More than six hundred years before, during the War of Reconquest, an army of Moors was besieging the city of Tarifa, on the strait of Gibraltar. The garrison commander, Alonso Pérez de Guzmán, called *the Good*, was ordered to surrender Tarifa as the price of his boy's life, who was held captive by the Moorish army. Guzmán the Good refused, and history says that he answered the renegade Christian conveying to him the message from the Moors, by flinging his dagger over the ramparts. Tarifa held out, relieved by a Christian fleet. But Guzmán's son had by then been killed by then.

By the early days of September, the Alcazar was still miraculously holding up, but the relentless bombardment by the besiegers' 6-inches guns began to produce substantial effects on the integrity of the fortress. With the north wall collapsed into rubble, the guns were turned towards the northeast tower. Attacks from the Santa Cruz Museum set fire to the already seriously damaged Government building, which finally burned down and was occupied by the attacking militia. Late in the following afternoon, a brilliant counterattack from the Alcazar led by Captain Varela regained the ruined building, little more now than large piles of ash-covered debris.

On Sunday the 6th a Nationalist airplane dropped several aluminum containers on the Alcazar. Two fell into the city, but one reached the Alcazar. It contained a letter from General Mola saying that the Nationalists were advancing from the North and from the South, and that General Yagüe's column had just taken Talavera de la Reina, very near Toledo. But this good news were soon met with grim bad news: engineer Lieutenant Barber reported to Moscardó that the enemy was digging two tunnels under the fortress, evidently in order to explode underground mines at strategic positions. The excavation was progressing rapidly and both tunnels could be expected to reach points directly under the Alcazar in about eight days.

Despite Red General Asensio's recent defeat near Talavera, Largo Caballero, the Head of Government of the Spanish Republic, had not lost confidence in him to take command of the siege of the Alcazar with the executive order: «Once and for all, the Toledan nightmare must be ended». Asensio's first task was to establish better discipline. He was a man of determination and ability, resolved to get a definitive victory for the Republic over the remaining heroic defenders. The day after his arrival, the northeast tower fell under the incessant cannon fire. Only two towers of the lofty structure were still standing.

On 8th September, at ten thirty in the evening, Major Vicente Rojo, at the service of the Republican Government, who had taught military history at the Alcazar Academy and was personally well known to Moscardó, asked on a megaphone (on the opposite side from the ruins of the Government building) for an hour's cease-fire the following day, in order to speak with Moscardó. After five minutes of consideration and consultation, Moscardó agreed.

And do you guarantee my personal safety? –asked Rojo–. We are gentlemen here, not like your Republican trash –replied heatedly Moscardó–. You may have an hour.

Largo Caballero had ordered Major Rojo to undertake these negotiations with the defenders because of the great world press attention by then being given to the siege, and because of the growing admiration for the courage of the defenders even among many Republican sympathizers. He wanted at least to try to get out the women and the children out, before the exploding mines would totally destroying the Alcazar –as nearly everybody believed–. Major Rojo presented terms in writing, obviously authorized by Largo Caballero: freedom for the women and children, and trial by the *people's courts* for all the fighting men in the garrison. In other words, the wives and children at the Alcazar were literally to purchase their lives with the lives of their husbands and fathers. Nobody, at the time, would put in doubt what would be the verdict of the *people's courts*.

We are willing to let the Alcazar become a cemetery, but not a dung heap! –was Moscardó's reply–. He wrote, however, an official answer on a scrap of paper:

Concerning the conditions for the surrender of the Alcazar, presented by the Committee, it gives me great pleasure to inform you that from the last soldier to the commander, they reject said conditions, and will continue to defend the Alcazar and the dignity of Spain to the end.

Major Rojo felt sympathy and admiration for his old comrade-in-arms. When he entered the room where Moscardó was, the Colonel refused to shake his hand. When, after the interview, Rojo turned his back on Moscardó, he suddenly turned and said: «Is there anything I can do for you?». «Yes – said Moscardó–. You can send us a priest. We want nothing else from you».

Some of the officers of the garrison crowded at that moment around Rojo, trying to draw information about the plans of the besiegers. He told them little, but they sensed his sympathy. Finally one asked him to join them. Rojo cast down his eyes and did not answer directly. Eventually, he said: «If I did, this very night my wife and my children in Madrid would be killed».

He left his pouch full of fine tobacco with them and, as he was blindfolded again to be led out, he suddenly cried «Viva España!».

Inside Moscardó was pacing the corridor up and down, and an aide was at his side. For a long time he was silent, then he said: «I just can't understand why a man of Rojo's integrity did not remain with us»... Minutes later, Moscardó burst again: «Do you think it would have been proper if I had shaken his hand? I wanted to do it, but I couldn't».

At the post office, Rojo handed over to Major Luis Barceló, head of the Defense Committee, Moscardó's defiant reply... Barceló, who was a very committed revolutionary, hurried to the nearest telephone: «Artillery batteries?... Fire night and day on the Alcazar!... Leave no stone larger than my little finger!».

The next evening, at ten o'clock, the besiegers sent another message by megaphone to the defenders. Canon Enrique Vázquez Camarasa, formerly ascribed to the cathedral of Madrid, with a well deserved reputation of being one of the most *progressive* high ranking clergymen in Spain, was announced. Approaching the Alcazar, Camarasa was met by Barceló and he exchanged the revolutionary clenched-fist salute with the militia at the battle line. His instructions were to take advantage of every opportunity to persuade the garrison to surrender.

Blindfolded, he was led inside the building. Captain Sanz de Diego, taking him roughly by his shoulders, asked: «Can you say Mass?». Camarasa muttered: «All right, if you wish»… Sensing his fear, one of the men standing nearby said: «Don't worry. It is that crowd out there that murders priests». The defenders of the Alcazar were not fools: They knew well what kind of priest would be allowed by the besiegers to enter the Alcazar.

With Moscardó in his office, Camarasa began a monologue about the happy life in Madrid. Churches were closed, but they were no longer burned down… His own house was protected by an anarchist guard. «Did you come prepared to confess us and celebrate Holy Mass? –asked Moscardó–. That is all we want!».

The homily was Camarasa's opportunity. In a few days, he said, the Alcazar would be blown up with everybody inside, including women and children. God would judge the men who allowed that to happen, the men responsible for the death of so many women and children... Some women began to sob, and some men were shaken. Finished the Mass, he baptized a just born child, and brought Holy Communion to the seriously wounded in the infirmary.

At Moscardó's office again, Camarasa argued once more that sacrificing the women and children was only stubbornness and vanity. Surely the women and children wanted to go! Moscardó's voice, rising as Camarasa's litany continued, replied: «No, señor; no, señor; no, señor!». The officers standing outside the door heard his repeated exclamation.

Then Moscardó called Carmen Romero de la Salamanca, daughter of one of his principal officers and wife of a Civil Guard Lieutenant. After listening to Camarasa's words, she said:

> Held here! That is a lie! I have talked with every woman in the Alcazar and all of them think as I do. Either we all leave here free, with our men and children, or else we will die with them in the ruins.

After that, Moscardó ordered Camarasa to be escorted out.

Two weeks later, Canon Camarasa left Spain for France. He was to survive the World War in Nazi-occupied France and died in 1946, despised by both sides.

On 14th September, the two tunnels reached the walls of the Alcazar. The sounds of the miners beneath the cellar floor could be heard by everyone. Moscardó ordered that everything in that part of the cellar be moved away and that barbed wire to be put around that part. Outside, the militia chanted: «Send out the women. It will soon be too late!». The next day, a four hour bombardment produced a long split in the east wall... That night, under the shadow of the impending detonation of the mines, Lieutenant Fernando Barrientos deserted... A military patrol in the city picked him up tried him and shot him on the spot.

On 18th September at 6:31 in the morning, the mine in the southwest side of the Alcazar exploded with a tremendous roar, heard in Madrid, some forty miles away. The one hundred foot northwest tower rose up towards the sky and crashed back to earth in a gigantic avalanche. The whole city of Toledo was covered by an enormous rolling cloud of black smoke. Fifteen minutes later, the main attack, 600 chosen men, charged from Zocodover Square, shouting: «We've killed the dogs! At them!». Looking through the rubble, sure of victory, they suddenly heard something totally unexpected: the high, clear notes of a bugle. The fifteen-year old trumpeter of the Alcazar was sounding the call to arms.

Within the Alcazar, a newcomer, a baby girl, delivered immediately after explosion, baptized later Josefa del Milagro (Josefa of the Miracle), joined the defenders that morning. The enormous adamantine crag upon which Toledo is built had proved tougher than anyone had imagined, confining the effects of the explosion to the area immediately above the mine... First scattered, then *in crescendo*, shouts of «Viva Cristo Rey!» came out of the defenders' quarters.

In the cellar, some of the women knelt facing the image of Blessed Virgin Mary, which, blown over, had been only slightly chipped. Colonel Moscardó himself joined them soon there.

* * *

On the night of 20th September, Largo Caballero himself arrived at Toledo demanding a take over of the Alcazar within 24 hours. Communist units, carrying the red hammer and sickle flags, attacked the next day, following the collapse under bombardment of the last of the four 100-foot towers. But they accomplished nothing. That was the day Franco decided that his main army advancing on Madrid must go first to relieve the Alcazar of Toledo. General Kindelán recalls his conversation with Franco:

> Do you know, General, that Toledo could cost us Madrid? –said Kindelán.
> Yes, I do –answered Franco–. I have meditated for a long time on the consequences of my decision... What would you do in my place?
> I would go for Toledo –replied Kindelán without hesitation– even if it meant not taking Madrid.
> Well, that's what I have decided –answered Franco.
> ...We must impress the enemy by convincing him that *whatever we propose to do, we achieve*, and that they can't do anything to stop it...

* * *

At dawn Sunday the 27th, a second mine was detonated under the Alcazar at the northern corner. The mine, smaller than the previous one, contained *only* one ton of TNT. General Varela and his men, seeing from afar, thought that, at the last moment, the besiegers had won... But, after a two hours battle, the defenders had won again, giving the lie to the false Government's announcement of its surrender that day.

Later that morning, seeing Varela's army «massing on the long barren hills to the north» (Hugh Thomas, *Spanish Civil War*, 2nd ed., p. 412), the garrison tied their gold and red traditional flag on a steel girder at the top of the pile of rubble in the northwest corner of the Alcazar. Furious, Major Barceló wanted to stay, but only a few men would stay with him.

At 6:40 in the evening, 20 Moroccan troops with Lieutenant Lahuerta, and five minutes later, 20 Spanish legionnaires with

Captain Teide, entered the city through an undefended back gate.

The next morning, 28th July, General Varela entered the Alcazar. Colonel Moscardó stepped forward and saluted him.

«Mi general, sin novedad en el Alcázar» (Nothing new at the Alcazar, my General!)».

Fr. Puyal, S.J., said Mass for the surviving defenders and Cardinal Gomá, Archbishop of Toledo, sent this message from Pamplona:

> Toledans: Our city and diocese have paid an enormous tribute of priestly lives. It is a glory and an infamy. Spaniards!, a glory because if our enemies have known how to kill, our priest have known how to die. In the clash of civilization against barbarism, of Hell against Christ [...], the banner-bearers of Christ (had to succumb the first) [...]. But among our sacrificed priests there has not been a single defection [...]. Glory to the martyrs! Honor to the Church which has such ministers!

The story of the Alcazar is an epic story destined to be remembered not only in the hearts and minds of the descendants of its 1936 defenders, but forever.

UNAMUNO AND MILLÁN ASTRAY

On 12th October 1936, in Salamanca, there took place a dramatic confrontation which became, in years to come, a symbol of the Spanish Civil War.

Salamanca is the site of the most famous Spanish university, founded by Alphonse X the Wise in the middle of the 13th century. In the 16th, the golden age of Spain, Francisco de Vitoria, Fray Luis de León and Domingo de Soto taught at Salamanca. Soto anticipated Galileo in describing correctly the accelerated motion of a heavy body falling to earth in free fall under the *uniformiter uniformis* attraction of the gravitational force.

The Chancellor of the university was at that dramatic moment, Don Miguel de Unamuno, one of the most respected and admired Spanish intellectuals of those troubled times. He was Professor of Greek, a poet, philosopher and novelist, profoundly Basque and profoundly Spanish. Unamuno had been an acerbic critic of Alphonse XIII's monarchy and of the dictatorship of Don Miguel Primo de Rivera. After supporting briefly the advent of the 2nd Republic, he had rejected, in no uncertain terms, its early anarchic tendencies, and since February 1936, the crimes promoted or consented by the government of the Popular Front.

Unamuno, in fact, had supported openly the civic-military rising of 18th July 1936, but, probably under the impression made by the ferocity unleashed by the war, he had begun to having second thoughts. Other Spanish intellectuals, such as Ortega, Marañón, Pérez de Ayala or Baroja, early sympathizers of the Republic in Madrid at the outbreak of the Civil War, seeing directly the revolutionary excesses committed in the Republican zone, had opted very soon, one after the other, to exile themselves. Many of them moved to Paris.

The academic celebration of 12th October, Day of the Race, as it was then called, would be presided over, as usual, in Salamanca by the University Chancellor. The arrival of General Millán Astray at the Assembly Hall of the University was not seen by some of those present as a good omen.

Robert Payne, in *The Civil War in Spain, 1936-1939* (New York, 1962, p. 111), describes the confrontation between Unamuno and Millán Astray as one between «the completely civilized man and the pure nihilist». In the account given by Payne, Luis Portillo, an eyewitness, does not hide where his sympathies lie. Millán Astray had lost an eye, an arm and a leg in Morocco, fighting for his country. But certainly he was no match for Salamanca's Chancellor as an orator.

On the other hand, at that moment, with half of Spain in arms against the other half, and with a Bolshevist revolution underway in Spain, for some of those present at the Assembly Hall it may not have been very clear who knew better what he was defending; who was the true enemy then of truth and freedom, and who was not.

On that 12th October, it was not contemplated in the program that Millán Astray was to speak. He was a soldier, not an orator. He had seen already many of his legionaries fall in combat. He knew the enemy, and probably he was convinced that many intellectuals who directly or indirectly had been fuelling the bloody conflict in Spain, did not really believe that there was anything worth fighting to death. Spaniards who continued to support the bloody Republic were for them guilty of treason.

They deserved death, «Viva la muerte!». Many in the audience roared «Arriba España!».

According to Portillo's description, Unamuno's response was impressive:

> All of you are hanging on my words. You all know me, and are aware that I am unable to remain silent. I have not learned to do so in the seventy-three years of my life. And I do not wish to learn it now anymore. At times, to be silent is to lie. For silence can be interpreted as acquiescence.
>
> It pains me to think that General Millán Astray should dictate here the pattern of mass psychology. That would be appalling. A cripple who lacks the spiritual greatness of Cervantes –a man, not a superman, virile and complete, in spite of his mutilations–, a cripple, I said, who lacks that loftiness of mind, is wont to seek ominous relief in seeing mutilation around him [...]. General Millán Astray would like to create Spain anew –a negative creation– in his own image and likeness. And for that reason he wishes to see Spain crippled as he unwittingly has made clear.

As Warren Carroll notes in «October» (*The Last Crusade*, p. 169), these words sound splendidly eloquent, but do they mean that Millán Astray wanted his legionaries killed or crippled? More than noble rhetoric, Unamuno's words can be recognized as a not too noble insult to a man who had lost an eye, an arm and a leg in the service of his country. Millán Astray's furious reply «Muera la inteligencia!» (Death to intelligence!) may have not been a rational response, but it can be surely understood as a spontaneous *impromptu* reaction to a vicious attack. José María Pemán, one of the most respected Nationalist intellectuals present, said at once: «No, long life to intelligence! Death to bad intellectuals!». The audience broke out in anger, some in support of Unamuno; some in support of Millán Astray.

Unamuno was still standing. Then his voice rang out again:

> This is the temple of the intellect, and I am its high priest. It is you who are profaning its sacred precincts.
>
> I have always been, whatever the proverb may say, a prophet in my own land. You will win, but you will not convince. You will win because you posses more than enough brute force, but you will not convince, because to convince means to persuade. And in order to persuade, you would need what you lack: reason and right in the

struggle. I consider it futile to exhort you to think of Spain. I have finished.

Don Miguel had said the last word. But he was fortunate to escape unharmed. In the audience were many who had seen enough innocent blood shed by the revolutionaries. Millán Astray's bodyguard was pointing his sub-machine gun at Unamuno and cries of anger were filling the assembly room. But, fortunately, Millán Astray was not an anarchist killer... His one good eye swept the room. He saw immediately the way out.

«Unamuno! –he said– Take the arm of the first lady!».

Doña Carmen Polo de Franco, the devoutly Catholic wife of Generalissimo Franco, responded immediately. In the words of a man in her escort who was there:

> Franco's wife stood up with an aloofness, an elegance which I doubt she could repeat. With one hand she gestured to the Legionary to deflect his sub-machine gun, and with the other, she took Don Miguel by the arm. Unamuno looked on the point of collapse. His head was sunk in his shoulders. With her other hand she made a gesture which we understood to mean she was summoning her guard. We formed up around the couple. Our lieutenant, perhaps on Doña Carmen's instructions, took up a position on Unamuno's other side and placed an arm round his shoulder. We had to use our rifle butts to control the spectators who pressed forward. There were shouts and cries... Franco's wife opened the door of her official car and told the lieutenant to take Unamuno home.

Apparently, few recent historians have noticed that it was Millán Astray himself who brought Carmen Franco to save Unamuno from the threatening crowd. He was not *nihilist*.

Let us ask a final rhetorical question. When the revolutionary masses began burning churches, killing innocent nuns and children in pre-Civil War Spain they had been warmed up for some time by brilliant and outspoken intellectuals, left-leaning republicans like Azaña, anarchists like García Oliver, socialists like Prieto or Largo Caballero, communists or Trotskyites like José Díaz or Andrés Nin. Were the crimes then committed the sole responsibility of the ignorant masses?

At the end, in Republican Spain, to cry «Viva España!» meant often a cruel death. To cry «Viva Rusia!», on the other hand, was met often with full acclaim.

At that time, the revolutionary masses were so gullible as to believe that nuns were giving poisoned caramels in the streets to the workers' children.

Yes, «Long life to good intellectuals!», but, «Beware of bad intellectuals!» too.

HISPANIA MARTIR

In the inauguration of the *Basilica of the Saint Cross of the Valley of the Fallen*, on 1st April 1959, Abbot Fray Justo Pérez de Urbel said the following:

> Tourists and pilgrims are astonished at seeing these imposing buildings and they leave here with the conviction that there is nothing like it in the world. «It is unique», exclaimed the primate of the Benedictine Order, and did not cease repeating that. «It is unbelievable», repeated a French prelate. A distinguished American summed up his impressions with these words: «It is the most marvelous thing I have ever seen». A member of the Roman Curia was reluctant to leave the basilica without having heard the prelude to *Parsifal* performed on the organ. I have seen more than one person crying in front of the Christ of the main altar, and a Protestant visitor falling on his knees, overwhelmed by such greatness.
>
> Such is the great monument our 20th century leaves side by side with the one left by the 16th in El Escorial; a surprising creation which it has been said will be proclaimed one of the great marvels of the European civilization.

And then there is the Cross, irradiating from the high its message of peace and reconciliation to all parts of Spain, facing that great plain where Spaniards will meet on the occasions of the great commemorations; and below, this unparalleled basilica for its greatness and for its beauty; with a dome which is an admirable synthesis of our religious history, with this Christ in the main altar, in front of which the coldest soul feels inclined to pray and to adore.

«And all this, what for?», asked a foreign magazine of worldwide circulation after describing, with half disguised amazement, the impressive greatness of the cross, the majesty of the basilica, and the fascinating beauty of the whole valley. This is, of course, a very natural question in those for whom there is nothing else beyond this material world.

He who comes here should come with faith and love; only then will he be able to understand when we explain to him: «This monument has been raised to God's glory, to God who deigned to come to us». This is the faith's answer. It was also built to proclaim the heroism and to honor the names and the mortal remains of those Brothers who gave their lives to leave us a country in peace, and to pray form them. This is the proof of our love.

People asking that question forget that a little more than twenty years ago two ideologies confronted each other on our soil with ferocious fury, filling every Spanish home with sorrow and mourning. Hundreds of thousands were left out in the streets, in the roads, in the fields, in the trees and rocks. For many of them nobody prayed; nobody honored their remnants; nobody gave them a sacred and blessed soil in which to rest. That Spain emerged victorious at last, that she knew how to unite the longings for progress with all the longings of the past: that Spain which works and prays, that Spain which forgets and forgives. If that Spain had been defeated, an immense dungeon crowned by the hammer and sickle, with a word emblematic of slavery and chaos: *Lenin*, would have emerged. But that was the Spain that won. And because of it, the moment of victory could be seen as a sign of peace and reconciliation.

Almost forty two years later, Pope John Paul II, in his homily at the papal chapel, said before the *Beatification* of *Servus Dei* José Aparicio Sanz, presbyter, and 233 companion martyrs at Saint Peter, in the Vatican, on 11th March 2001:

On several occasions I have reminded you of the need to preserve the memory of the martyrs. They are the most eloquent proof of the faith's truth, which knows how to give a human face even to the most violent death, and manifests its beauty even in the middle of the most atrocious suffering. It is therefore necessary that the particular churches make every effort to keep alive the memory of those who have suffered that martyrdom.

My good friend José Francisco Guijarro, author of *Persecución Religiosa y Guerra Civil, 1936-1939*, gives an excellent summary of the events surrounding the *shooting* of the *Monument to the Sacred Heart of Jesus* in the *Cerro de los Angeles*. The restored monument is located at the center of the Iberian Peninsula, very close to the capital of Spain. On 18th July 1936, in the afternoon, about thirty members of the Congregation of Workers of Saint Joseph and the Sacred Heart of Jesus arrived at the *Cerro de los Angeles* to do the customary vigil of nocturnal adoration before the Blessed Sacrament. When the Mass was finished, already in the morning of the 19th, Sunday, Fidel de Pablo García, leading member of Catholic Action in the parish of Espíritu Santo, 29 years age, came back to Madrid, accompanying the priest who had just celebrated Mass, don José María Vegas Pérez, chaplain of the Monument to the Sacred Heart of Jesus, with most other participants in the vigil. Only five remained at the Monument, confident in the imminent arrival of the troops just rebelled against the Republic. The *guard of honor* to the Sacred Heart would not be interrupted. The five components of this *guard of honor* were Pedro Justo Dorado Dellmans (31 years old), Fidel Barrio Muñoz (21), Elías Requejo Sorondo (19), carpenter specialist, from the Youth of Catholic Action of the parish of Espíritu Santo; Blas Ciarreta Ibarrondo (40), married with Ángela Pardo, who had arrived recently with his wife in Madrid from Santurce (Vizcaya), and Vicente de Pablo García (19), carpenter, brother of Fidel who had left with the chaplain and the others.

They remained there alone for some time, and after militiamen arrived at the *Cerro de los Angeles* to dislodge the Carmelite Nuns from the Monastery, they remained in the surroundings. Thereafter, they went to a country house near Las Zorreras, belonging to the nearby village of Perales del Río.

After having lunch, they paid for their lunch to the servants in the country house and offered them to pay for their lodgings during the few days they expected to stay there, waiting the imminent arrival of the troops who had just rebelled against the Republic. At last, some of them went on the morning of the 23rd to the village of Perales del Río. They had breakfast in a tavern and blessed the food with the sign of the cross before beginning to eat, something which was obviously seen by others present. This might well have signed their death sentence. According to contemporary reports, the main cause of militia-men coming soon thereafter to assassinate them was having seen them praying the rosary and blessing the food before eating. It is believed that they were denounced by Honorato Pérez, in charge of the country house. In the morning of the 23rd, militia-men from Marañosa came to detain the so-called *friars in disguise*. The wife and daughters of Honorato greeted the militia enthusiastically, and a parody of trial took place in which the young men had to suffer all kinds of vexations. Then, facing the Monument of the Sacred Heart, not yet blown up, all of them were shot. They died crying «Viva Cristo Rey!». The Sacred Heart of Jesus seemed to give His blessing from the high to these five workers. Later it was reported that one of the young men's bodies had fallen down with the arms open, making a cross, and that it was necessary afterwards to break them in order to fit the body within the coffin. The executioners came down to the church at the nearby village after the murders, tore down all images and sacred ornaments, and burned out everything at 10:00 am, that 23rd July 1936.

The priest who had said that last Mass after the night prayer vigil and his companion were soon murdered also. The priest was taken out of the jail of San Antón, in which he had taken refuge, thinking it was safer to be in jail that remaining in the street in those terrible days, and on 27th November 1936, he was executed in Paracuellos del Jarama. Vicente de Pablo, Fidel's brother, was detained on 26th August 1936, by militia-men of the Communist party, and brought to the *checa* located at O'Donnell 22, accused of being guilty of Catholic ideals as a prominent *requeté*. From O'Donnell he was brought up to the *checa* of San Bernardo, where he was questioned and tortured till 8th September, the day on which he was shot at Km 7 of the road to Valencia. The report says that no more details about his death are known.

On 4th October 1936, the Revolutionary Committee of Getafe detained and shot ten members of Catholic Action belonging to the parish of Saint María Magdalena. Its President, Juan Benavente Butragueño (24), had been shot already in the outside of Getafe's jail on 23rd August. Ten young Catholic Action members of that parish in Getafe, very near the *Cerro de los Angeles*, were shot on 4th October and their bodies were abandoned that night. The following day, the bodies were identified and brought to the burial place of Santa Isabel Street.

The bloody events at the surroundings of the Monument to the Sacred Heart near Madrid are only illustrative of events taking place then all over the Iberian Peninsula under the misgovernment of the Republic in those terrible summer days of 1936. Such an anti-religious fury is difficult to understand.

* * *

During the ten days of the 1936 October revolution in Asturias, 46 priests and religious men had been murdered. Largo Caballero and Indalecio Prieto's Socialist party had been sliding since then more or less openly towards the Bolshevist revolutionary model. The Communists had absorbed the revolutionary youth branch of the Socialist party, and were confident of taking soon charge of the Popular Front. A revolutionary take-over was expected to materialize before October 1936. The assassination of Calvo Sotelo, on the other hand, precipitated the rising of 18th July 1936. And in the long Civil War of 1936-39, the 46 priests and religious murdered just in ten days in 1934 became 6,300 priests and religious murdered in three years. There would have been undoubtedly substantially more if the war had been won by the Communist dominated Popular Front.

According to Hugh Thomas, in no other short period of European history, and possibly of world history, there has been such a passionate murderous hate unleashed.

The list of Catholic Bishops martyred is an impressive one, most of them in the short period from July to December 1936 (see Antonio Montero, *Historia de la Persecución Religiosa en España*, B.A.C., Madrid, 1961).

- **Msgr. Nieto (Bishop of Sigüenza):** Martyred on 27th July, 1936. He died crying «Viva España!» and «Viva Cristo Rey!». His body was thrown down to a gorge and recovered there by the nationalists a few days later.
- **Msgr. Huix (Bishop of Lérida):** Martyred on 5th August 1936. At his request, he was the last to be shot in his group, so as to be able to give absolution to the last of his companions.
- **Msgr. Laplana (Bishop of Cuenca):** Martyred on 8th August 1936. His last words to the executioners were «You can kill me. My body I leave with you, but my soul will go to heaven... I forgive you and will pray for you from heaven».
- **Msgr. Asensio (Bishop of Barbastro):** Martyred on 9th August 1936. According to eyewitnesses, in spite of the insults of his murderers, he walked up with admirable countenance to his execution, and died blessing them.
- **Msgr. Serra (Bishop of Segorbe):** Martyred on 9th August 1936. These were his last words: «You can kill me, but you cannot stop me blessing you».
- **Msgr. Basulto (Bishop of Jaén):** Martyred on 12th August 1936. His last words were: «Lord, forgive me my sins and forgive those who kill me». His sister Teresa, who was to be shot with him, said: «This is an infamy». To which the murderers responded: «Don't worry: You will be killed by a woman». And Josefa Coso, a militia-woman, came forward and shot her in cold blood.
- **Msgr. Borrás (Bishop of Tarragona):** Martyred on 12th August 1936. He died blessing his assassins. They put firewood on his still warm body and set fire to it.
- **Msgr. Estenaga (Bishop of Ciudad Real):** Martyred on 22nd August 1936. He died blessing his assassins. Offered in advance by his people the possibility of escaping, he said: «...The shepherd must not go away; my duty is to remain here».
- **Msgr. Ventaja (Bishop of Almeria):** Martyred on 30th August 1936. Shot, sprinkled with gasoline, burned and

left lying on the ground, until he was buried by neighbors some days later.

- **Msgr. Medina Olmos (Bishop of Guadix):** Martyred the same day. Also shot, sprinkled with gasoline and burned.
- **Msgr. Irurita (Bishop of Barcelona):** The rising of General Goded in Barcelona, on 21st July, took place when he was saying Mass at the Episcopal chapel. He had time to come out with his aide through a back door. Don Antonio Tort, a good Catholic merchant, generously requested that the Bishop come home with him and his family. A few months later a militia-men on patrol found Msgr. Irurita, that had been receiving discretely priests and religious women *de incognito* and detained him together with don Antonio, who paid with his own life for the brave act of charity of which he was guilty.
- **Msgr. Polanco (Bishop of Teruel)** (who deserves special mention): Martyred on 7th January 1938, a few days before the Nationalist troops entered Barcelona, in the final weeks of the Civil War. Msgr. Polanco had been consecrated Bishop of Teruel just before the outbreak of the war. He had signed in 1937 the Collective Letter of the Spanish Bishops to all the Bishops of the world, defending the justice of the Nationalists' cause from the false accusations in the international press. The successful offensive of the red army at Christmas 1937 took Teruel, which was dangerously located in a salient of the fire line. Msgr. Antoniutti, delegate of the Holy See in the Nationalist zone, suggested Msgr. Polanco should leave the city; he refused however. When Teruel was taken, the case of Msgr. Polanco, undersigner of the Collective Letter, was followed up with great interest by the war correspondents of the International press. Msgr. Polanco was invited to withdraw his signature from the Collective Letter, but he refused in the following terms:

There is in the letter doctrine and there are facts. 1st) As far as doctrine is concerned, it is the doctrine of the Church, and I have nothing to rectify. 2nd) As far as the facts are concerned, errors are still possible, no matter how diligently or objectively researched, in some figure or some data perhaps, which would never impair the main thesis. So, if you prove to me that there is some error, I would gladly admit it, but, in its place, I may put other facts of which I have been eyewitness, like the red crimes in the Albaicín, which I cannot and should not ignore.

At the end of the Civil War, in the confusion of the last hours, a truck of the red army under command of Pedro Díaz as political commissar, arrived in Can Bosch, near the French frontier and picked up Bishop Polanco and Colonels Barba and Rey d'Harcourt, leaders of the defense of Teruel, who had finally surrendered the city to the red army. The Bishop and the two Colonels were machine-gunned on 7th February 1939, near the dry course of the Muga river.

To this list of martyred Bishops we should add the name of Dr. Ponce, Apostolic Administrator of the Diocese of Orihuela, and therefore acting Bishop there, who was shot on 30th November 1936, by the wall of Elche's cemetery. His last words were, according to his biographer, «What a happiness!», «From this road to heaven!».

The full list of martyred priests was, and still is, impressive: 4,184 secular priests murdered out of a total of 19,546 in the various Spanish Dioceses (21.4 %). In Madrid-Alcalá, 334 (29.8 %); in Valencia, 327 (27.2 %); in Tortosa, 316 (61.9 %); in Toledo, 286 (47.6 %); in Barcelona, 279 (22.3 %), and so forth.

The list of martyred religious and nuns is as follows:

Men: Agustinians, 155; Claretians, 259; Dominicans, 132; Escolapians, 204; Franciscans, 226; Brothers of La Salle, 165; Jesuits, 115; Marist Brothers, 176; other, 943. Total: 2,365. Women: Adoratrices, 26; Capuchins, 20; Discalced Carmelites, 26; Concepcionists, 10; Sisters of the Christian Doctrine, 17; Sisters of Charity, 30; Missionaries of Saint Francis of Paula, 9; other, 145. Total: 283.

No definitive statistics of martyred men and martyred women belonging to lay organizations such as Catholic Action, Franciscan or Dominican Third Orders, Marian Congregations, etc., have been made to date; but many cases of exemplary bravery and piety have been recorded. Of course, in principle, they should outnumber considerably those of martyred priests and religious.

* * *

The great French Catholic poet Paul Claudel said it well:

Heaven and Hell are put into your hand and you have forty seconds to choose!

Forty seconds –too long! Sister Spain, holy Spain, you have chosen!

Eleven bishops, sixteen [see below] priests massacred and not a single apostasy!

Ah! Might I like you one day rise my voice to testify in the splendor of noontide.

(Paul Claudel, «Aux Martyrs Espagnols»).

The actual figure of martyred priests is six thousand (6,832), not sixteen thousand, as wrongly given by Paul Claudel.

CAPTAIN CORTÉS, DEFENDER OF SANTA MARÍA DE LA CABEZA

Jaén: 1936.

According to J. Arrarás (*Historia de la Cruzada Española*, pp. 348-427), the Marxist forces in Jaén were about 5,000 militia-men of the Unified Socialist Youth (mostly socialists with some communists) plus about 5,000 syndicalists (UGT and FAI); the counter revolutionary forces were much less, perhaps 15%, made up of about 300 from *Falange Española*, 200 *Requetés*, 200 from the Agrarian Federation and a few hundred partly committed members of *Acción Popular*, the Christian Democratic party winner in the previous 1933 elections, which had lost later in the February 1936 elections. The Civil Guard, supposed to keep law and order at any time, independently of the governing political faction, had about 800 men in six companies stationed in the province, at Jaén (capital), Linares, Úbeda, Andújar, Martos y Villacarrillo.

At the beginning of 1936, Captain Santiago Cortés González had been assigned to the Civil Guard Command in Jaén. He was preceded by an aureole of prestige, because he had confronted the revolutionary leaders at Mancha Real in October 1934, the first revolutionary coup launched by socialists, anarchists and separatists against the duly elected conservative government.

In the months previous to the civil-military rising of 18th July, the head of the Civil Guard Command in Jaén was Lieutenant Colonel Pablo Martínez Iglesias (a good man but timid and undecided). With him were Commandants Eduardo Nofuentes (also somewhat timid and undecided) and Ismael Navarro (with clear left-leaning sympathies). On the other hand, Captains Santiago Cortés, Miguel Amezcua and José Rodríguez de Cueto (supernumerary), lieutenant Manuel Rueda, second lieutenants José Carbonell, Antonio Cabeza and Francisco del Amo, and sub-officers José de Vicente Zamorano, Santiago Fuentes, Romualdo Hortelano, Vifredo Casares with a few more (either temporarily discharged or absent) were all certainly not in doubt about what was their duty in those critical times.

The month of June 1936 was a terrible one in Jaén: ripe grain fields on fire, assaults to private properties and revolutionary farmers brandishing axes and sickles. Three men came together in *hotel Francia* to ponder the situation: Ramón Lendínez and Ángel Madrid (Falangists), and Santiago Cortés. Expecting a civil-military rising for 10th July, they examined plans for an armed rebellion against the Marxist abuses. At dawn on 10th July, they informed the members of the local junta that no password had yet been received for the rising that day. The civil rebels were uneasy. Within the Civil Guard an underground confrontation was developing between the officers who were ready to join the rising, and some of their unwilling higher rank superiors. The spirit of the rank and file Civil Guards could have been more favorable to the rising. Young revolutionaries were coming every day to the quarters of the Civil Guard singing hostile couplets.

On 13th July Calvo Sotelo, the leader of the Monarchist group in the parliament, was assassinated in Madrid. The murder galvanized all the non-Marxist half of Spain. 18th July arrived and the Popular Front reacted immediately.

In Jaén, the Civil Government was under heavy pressure. The *Casa del Pueblo* was then reaching a point of no return. The Socialist representative Peris Caruana took up the governing authority in Jaén bypassing the legal governor, Mr. Zanón. Deputy Peris Caruana made a phone call to Madrid saying: «In Jaén everything is under control». But this was not true; Jaén had by then all the appearance of a city taken over by the mobs. The leaders of *Falange* and the *Requetés* had been detained and had been put into jail.

When the rising of Africa's Army became known in Jaén, the officers and rank and file at the Command of Civil Guard showed clear signs of willingness to support it, but those higher up in command (Iglesias, Nofuentes and Navarro) subdued the enthusiasm of their men. Lieutenant Colonel Iglesias asked for time to ponder the situation. But the officers constituted themselves in *permanent council*. Iglesias decided somehow to follow orders... But that decision fell like a bombshell among the officers. Tension mounted during the whole of the afternoon and the early night of 18th July. Cortés still hopped to reverse the attitude of his superior. At the end, Iglesias said he understood the wish of his officers to join the Army of Africa, but added that he would like to know first the orders from Madrid. Navarro and Nofuentes refused to join the rising.

Meanwhile, all the revolutionary elements began to concentrate at the Casa del Pueblo. They declared a *general strike*. Very soon, San Francisco square was swarming with people. Voices asking arms for the people increase and in many homes belonging to peaceful citizens, people began to accept that the rising had failed. But people listening to *Radio Sevilla* were hearing the addresses of the Madrid Government, when, suddenly, the broadcast stopped... After a few minutes. a calm and solemn voice was heard saying: «Don Gonzalo Queipo de Llano, Jefe de la Segunda Región Militar: Hago saber...». The decree proclaiming martial law in Seville and its demarcation followed... Falangist groups in Jaén went onto the streets, but hesitations in the Civil Guard Headquarters were still going on.

Arms were given to some revolutionary peasants. The revolutionaries began to occupy the most strategic parts of the city. The *Episcopal Palace* was assaulted by the mob, which expected to find there arms for the *fascists* but finds none. The Civil Government, in the meantime, forced Lieutenant Colonel Iglesias to give more arms to the people. There were cases, like that of the Caporal Pedro Vivas Chabernas, in charge of the post at Fuente del Río, where the local authority flatly refused to order the giving of arms to the mob. Caporal Vivas Chabernas confiscated the documents shown by the political delegate containing authorization to take up the arms, and sent him away in no uncertain terms.

Organized from the *Casa del Pueblo*, terror began to spread out in Jaén capital. The Church of La Merced was assaulted. The Convent of the Missionaries of the Heart of Mary was likewise attacked. Many religious were martyred and the church was sacked. Any hope that Jaén would join the rising of the African Army seemed lost. The whole province was soon coming under Marxist control and the various jails became overflowing with suspected sympathizers of the civic-military rising.

What was the Civil Guard doing in the meantime? The struggle between Lieutenant Colonel Iglesias and his officers went on and on. The decision of Iglesias to follow the orders of the Government of the Popular Front was confronted by serious objections of the officers to give arms to the revolutionary mob, whose criminal intentions were more than evident. The Civil Guards firmly opposed the idea that arms being given to the revolutionary rabble.

Then the Socialist leaders threatened to attack the Civil Guard quarters if arms were not forthcoming. Iglesias panicked and agreed with the acting Civil Governor to put together at the capital all Civil Guards scattered through the province. The concentration takes place without incidents. Among the officers concentrated in Jaén was Captain Rodríguez de Cueto, who had been discharged previously by the Popular Front because of his determined actions confronting revolutionary activity. He joined the Civil Guards concentrated in the capital.

Rodríguez de Cueto and Cortés still expected to convince Iglesias to let the Civil Guards in Jaén join the civic-military rising, but commandant Navarro objected.

In the meantime, 50 Civil Guards crossed the battle lines not too far from Jaén and joined the rebel Nationalist forces at

Cordova. In Jaén, the bishop, Msgr. Basulto Jiménez, was taken prisoner by revolutionary peasants, who proceeded to despoil the Episcopal residence. The Cathedral was sacked. Another large group of 150 Civil Guards joined the Nationalists. The first infamous *tren de la muerte* (train of the death), packed with 325 arrested civilians, left the city and headed towards Madrid. At the Atocha station in the Spanish capital, a revolutionary mob tried to set fire to the train. 280 prisoners were shot on the spot. Another train left for Madrid with 300 on board. At Atocha, the mob attacked it and shot the passengers including the Bishop of Jaén and his sister. Msgr. Basulto as already mentioned died forgiving his enemies.

In Andújar, Captain Reparaz had held firm against the violent revolutionary mob and had given orders to fire in self-defense at the aggressors, resulting in six dead. The revolutionary leaders asked that he be immediately shot. But he was finally ordered to join the republican column of General Miaja, sent by the Popular Front to recover Cordova and managed to defect to the nationalists.

To the Sanctuary of Santa María de la Cabeza: Cortés in command

Eventually, on 16th August the local authorities gave permission to the Civil Guards and families concentrated in Jaén to move to the Sanctuary of Santa María de la Cabeza, about 30 km from Jaén, and to Lugar Nuevo, a nearby location.

First by railroad and then by trucks, about 1,200 persons, including Civil Guards, their wives and children, some carabineers and other civilian personnel, moved in a orderly fashion to the Sanctuary on 16th August. Cortés went with his two eldest boys, leaving the little ones in Jaén with his wife.

Arrarás gives a vivid account of the sufferings and the incredible vicissitudes of this group of men, women and children under siege for eight months, surrounded by forces outnumbering the men at the Sanctuary by fourteen to one. This was an odyssey comparable only to that of the Alcazar of

Toledo, but much longer and, at the end, with very little or no hope of being rescued by the Nationalists.

Only a brief outline can be given here.

On 19th August Lieutenant Colonel Iglesias received orders to go to Madrid. Cortés pointed out to him when he was leaving, the bad impression produced on the Civil Guards who saw in this a maneuver of the Popular Front Government. Two days later, with Iglesias in Madrid, Nofuentes was in command at the Sanctuary…

Cortés said farewell to Captain Rodríguez de Cueto, who, as Captain Reparaz did a few days before, left the Sanctuary to try to join the Nationalists in Cordova. He hoped to be able to defend the Sanctuary until it was liberated by the Nationalists. For the moment they had some food, there was abundant hunting in the surroundings, and it was still possible to buy food from the nearby peasants.

On 26th August a group of 50 Civil Guards from Linares joined those at the Sanctuary.

However, the following day a truck full of red revolutionaries from Andújar, where they had been shooting *enemies of the people*, approached the Sanctuary with a long list of prospective victims.

On 31th August Nofuentes seemed to say that he was ready to surrender the Sanctuary to the revolutionary mob. Cortés disagreed violently. Supported by the remaining officers, he said: «Those willing to go out of the Sanctuary should go out now». Nofuentes and a reduced group left the Sanctuary. In their flight, the revolutionaries passed close to a nearby spring, where some women of the Civil Guards were washing their clothes. They stopped and attempted to abuse them within sight of those in the Sanctuary. This made clear to everybody the worth of promises by the revolutionaries to respect the men and women if they were to surrender.

For weeks, the red radios kept broadcasting the surrender of Santa María de la Cabeza. The defenders did not at the time whether the Nationalist authorities in Seville and Cordova knew that they were still holding out against all odds at the Sanctuary. At last, on 25th September, a Civil Guard and a plain clothed comrade from the Sanctuary arrived at Cordova and told the authorities there that in Santa María were 150 Civil Guards, about 900 civilians, women and children, with little food to resist a prospective long siege. Nearby, 60 Civil Guards with 300 family and civilians were holding out at Lugar Nuevo, close to the Sanctuary. On 29th September the Nationalists sent a small plane to take a close look to the site. They reported that they had seen a large Spanish flag and a big panel with the word *Auxilio*.

In subsequent flights, the Nationalists succeeded in sending safely a few *messenger* doves to the group at the Sanctuary.

On 25th October, the open field surrounding the Sanctuary was full with an expectant multitude watching eagerly the liberation of two doves with a message for General Queipo de Llano.

First message from Captain Cortés
to General Queipo de Llano

Camp of the *Virgen de la Cabeza*, 25th October 1936.

To his Excellence D. Gonzalo Queipo de Llano:

My respected and dear General: I have no words to describe the scene in this camp when your patriotic letter of 7th October [...], was read before the armed forces and before the blessed Virgin at this Sanctuary. With tears in my eyes I spoke to those, sharing pain and bitterness for more than two months already; men, women, children and elderly, all cried with gratitude feeling the protection of the Fatherland through your letter.

As an account of what has happened since 18[th]August, the day on which we moved to his Sanctuary, I must say that I put an end to my sickness leave and talked with Captain Reparaz, who was ready to be sent with the Marxists to the Cordova's front. We agreed about his immediate move to Cordova, and to the uprising of the rest of our forces, with their families, to station at this promontory where we are. On the 21st, Lieutenant Colonel don Pablo Iglesias departed for Madrid, following orders of the Government, and appointed Commandant to don Eduardo Nofuentes. On the 25th, the said chief in command, after a violent exchange with me, and, against my unbending opposition, gave the only *Hotchkiss* machine gun we had to the Marxists, with fifty nine rifles and fifteen thousand cartridges. On the 29th we had knowledge of the arrival at Cordova of our fellows in arms through the airplanes of our Army flying over our positions.

On 2nd September, I wrote down a letter, [finally] signed by our commandant with the unanimous consent of all officers, in which we made clear our breaking relations with the delegate of the Governor. At that time the siege of our camp began with Artillery, Assault forces and militia.

On the 12th, the red Air Force came in order to compel us to surrender; from this moment I had to have a continuous battle with our commander, who was willing to surrender our position, and tried to let a red committee enter and proceed to the dismissal of the Civil Guard, to which I not only objected but I swore it would not happen under my responsibility; in spite of it, in the morning of the 14th, after one thousand difficulties raised by me, he agreed to the surrender and evacuation, in my absence.

Providence determined that, thanks to a handful of brave young men accompanying me all the time, we were able to shortcut the evacuation, already underway, and to stop seven Assault Guards and four militia men in their flight. I took the command of the armed force from that very moment. Immediately I organized the Company, with the brave officers, First Lieutenant don Manuel Rueda; Second Lieutenant don José Carbonell; First Lieutenant of Carabineers, don Juan Porto, and I gave the command of the company to Captain don Manuel Rodríguez, who had presented himself to me later. On the 15th an intense bombardment by the red Air Force began until the 24th. More than four hundred bombs were dropped, which, due to the irregularities of the terrain and to the protection of our Virgin, produced only a few casualties; thereafter, menaces, bombardments and fusillades alternated, with variable intensity, until the 9th, on which the precarious situation with the food reserves became critical, and our Air Force came to recognize it. On the 10th the firing upon us kept going on. Our airplanes threw us food for only one day. On the 13th, more food came from the air; the messenger doves sent to us crashed on the irregular terrain; two Sergeants and three Civil Guards from the enemy camp joined us. On the 13th I made contact with our forces in Lugar Nuevo, commanded by the brave officer don Francisco Ruano, who kept very high the spirit of our troops. On the 22nd (early in the morning) forced by the desperate food situation, I ordered the incursion of a group of sixty men commanded by an officer, into the surrounding camp held out by the enemy, and they were successful in bringing back with them wheat, chickpeas, and cattle for fifteen days; at the end, the Nationalist Air Force appeared again with food for two days, and two of the doves which were carrying this message came back safely to our hands; we had at our disposal a continuous electric current generator and a deficient radio receiver, and were yet able of hearing your talks with indescribable satisfaction following the advance of our glorious Army. We still have gasoline to feed the motor to listen the radio about ten days; we need a machine gun; please, send us defensive sandbags to protect us from the attacks of the enemy air force. We need winter clothes, especially for the women and the children, and blankets for the force on duty. The food should be deposited on the little plaza formed by the group of houses to avoid waste; food falling on high slopes over the rocks is lost more than fifty per cent; for the moment we can manage without bread and chickpeas, we prefer codfish, conserves, coffee, sugar, sausages and powdered milk for the sick children; sanitary material, disinfectant specially, injections for breast, heart and hemorrhages. From the front facade of the Sanctuary to a metallic post with a little flag there will be a purse with our mail, to be picked up from the plain with a hook. We have dynamite but no tools to use it for defense against the enemy's air force [...]. With respect to the good spirits of our soldiers I am proud to say that they all respond like one man since I have taken charge of the position; they are ready to die with me if necessary rather than falling into the hands of that rabble surrounding us. When I left [Jaén] I left there my wife sick, three children, a little boy born after my leaving (I don't know him yet); my fathers and my brothers (one in jail), I am afraid they may be abused; please, keep anonymous my name and those of others in this armed forces until the takeover of the said capital [Jaén]... And that is all, my General. Confident the protection of our beloved brunette Virgin who takes care of us, and also confident of the bravery of our Army, all of us here feel proud of being Spanish more than ever, and all will know how to respond accepting as all sacrifices which await us till the hour of our liberation.

S.S.S. and subordinated Santiago Cortés González. *Signed.* To the physician who takes care of us, I send you the strong embrace of all us. To my uncle don Matías Cortés, Plaza del Duque 8, my strong embrace.

From this first message on 25th October 1936 to his last short message on 27th April 1937, reproduced below, six months of incredible heroism and suffering testify to the faith and patriotism of those men, women and children under siege at the Sanctuary of Santa María de la Cabeza, and at the nearby position of Lugar Nuevo. J. Arrarás, in his *Historia de la Cruzada Española*, tells it well. It cannot be told properly here.

On April 27th 1937, Captain Cortés, only a few days before his heroic death, wrote his last message:

Guardia Civil, Comandancia de Jaén, Capitán P. Jefe Accidental.

Sir:

At this moment I see ten tanks approaching this encampment, at 2 pm, the enemy found no other way to achieve his sinister purposes. The *messenger* doves sent away to you this morning are still over the debris of this Sanctuary; with the same faith, as a Christian and as a patriot in all my actions, I dare again to address V. E., informing you about these facts in case there is still time to send the aid I have been requesting for a such a long time.

I am not asking for my life, I know my life is worth little, but I ask for the lives of these 1,200 innocents who are begging and not giving up in their hope of liberation.

May God guard V. E. for many years.

Camp of the Sanctuary, 27th April 1937.

The Captain.

Signed: Santiago Cortés.

To his Excellencies the Generalissimo of the Nationalist Army, and to the General in Chief of the Army of the South, and Military Governor of Cordova.

The final massive assault on the Sanctuary took place on 1st May. The red artillery concentrated fire on the North watershed. The defenders saw the tanks approaching. They tried to stop them with hand grenades, unsuccessfully. Cortés, still at his post of command, surrounded by ruins, smoke and dust, sent his last heliographic message: *Resistance impossible. Help from Air Force, quickly.*

Cortés, who had received already two lesser wounds, fell finally, under the rubble, mortally wounded. José Liébana, the heroic medical student who had served as an improvised surgeon during the long siege, was with him. When Rueda arrived,

Liébana, with tears in his eyes, said: «My Lieutenant, our Captain is mortally wounded». When the attackers came in, they evacuated Cortés in an ambulance in order to avoid possible incidents with the revolutionary mob. Dr. Laguna intervened surgically and Captain Cortés lasted only a few hours. His son testified that during those four hours his father was continually subject to interrogation by chiefs of the red Army. They surely must have tried to extract a written declaration from him saying that he was wrong. But after such a long heroic resistance against the elements, it is utterly unlikely that Captain Cortés would have signed freely such a declaration.

* * *

The famous *Law of Historic Memory*, voted by Zapatero's Government in his first term in office, will be remembered hopefully as a very stupid attempt to rewrite history in reverse seventy years after the facts.

A visitor to the ruins of the Sanctuary left written there, on 4th December 2008, the following comment:

It is really impressive to the Crypt where Captain Cortés rests, truly that place has *something special…* It can be breathed in the air and in the landscape. Every honest Spaniard who visits that place should say a prayer for the souls of those who were there under siege and specially for Captain Cortés… for his heroic sacrifice in defense of faith and freedom confronting the lawlessness of the red yoke.

DECORATED CITIES
(Pamplona, Valladolid, Oviedo, Seville)

A handful of Spanish cities deserved at the Civil War the *Laureada de San Fernando*, the highest collective decoration of the Spanish Army for courage in decisive actions.

Pamplona: On 14th July, General Mola formally accepted the conditions of the Carlist leaders to join the forthcoming military rising. The *requetés*, as the Navarrese carlists were known, were a formidable potential fighting force, heirs of their namesakes who had fought (unsuccessfully) for God, Fatherland and *Fueros* (Rights) at three wars in the previous century. Ancient Carlist King pretender Alfonso Carlos, from Vienna, gave his full support.

The rising in Pamplona was set for Sunday 19th July, one day after the military rising. The *Requeté* was ordered to recognize officers of the regular army rebelling against the republican Government fighting under the historic red and gold banner. The night before, word went out that every *requeté* with arms should be next morning in Pamplona's main square. All during that night, with exultation in their faces, they streamed to Plaza del Castillo from the surrounding hills and valleys. Many *requetés*, like the Catholic Army of the Vendeé after the French Revolution, wore Sacred Heart badges on their shoulders or on their hearts. Some villages of Navarra were virtually depopulated of men. Artajona sent 775 of its 800 men. Records of enlisted men show as many as eight members of the same family. A well known story from the war tells that one man, when he was asked who should be told if he were killed in action, responded: «José María Hernandorena, of the Tercio of Montejurra, age 65. He is my father». And if he should be killed too?: «Then, José María Hernandorena, of the Tercio of Montejurra, age 15. He is my son». (See Juan Urra Lusarreta, Madrid, 1967, quoted in Warren Carroll, *The Last Crusade*, Front Royal, 1996).

By 23rd July, there were 20,000 Navarrese volunteers in service. General Mola was able to begin sending them out immediately in all directions. Five hundred men helped to take Logroño, taken almost without resistance. Twelve hundred *requetés* went to Saragossa. Alava, one of the Basque Provinces, had been secured by three thousand *requetés* on 19th July. In Burgos, the capital of Old Castile, *requetés* who had prayed the rosary together the night before marched in to help Colonel Gavilán to take the city. Burgos was soon to become the capital of Nationalist Spain.

Valladolid: *Falange Española*, headed in Valladolid by Onésimo Redondo, was particularly strong in that old Castilian city at the outbreak of the Civil War. Its leader, proceeding from the ACN de P(Asociación Católica Nacional de Propagandistas), insisted that the movement should make explicit «the utmost respect for the (Catholic) religious tradition of our people». In contrast with Mussolini's Fascism, which exalted the State with reference to the Roman Empire, Falange-JONS did it with reference to the Christian Spanish Empire, and defended explicitly social justice and workers rights against the excesses of Marxism and Capitalism.

Onésimo had been in jail since 25th June, with eighteen young Falangists. At a recent meeting with university students and members of the SEU (the Falangist Students Syndicate) he had said: «Moscow is ready to take hold of our fatherland. *Falange* is vigilant and will announce without hesitation the decisive moment.. Then, neither books, nor girlfriends, nor parents, nor home will stop us». On 16th July, General Saliquet came up from Madrid to Valladolid to head the uprising. The Falangist elements in town were very active. In short order, the CNT (Anarchist Syndicate), the Post Office and the Local Radio Station were occupied. Martial Law was declared, and all imprisoned Falangists were liberated. The Socialist Center (*Casa del Pueblo*) was dislodged and the civil authorities loyal to the Republic were summarily court-martialed.

Republican forces had reached on the 21st the strategically important Somosierra Pass, connecting Valladolid with Madrid. A large Republican column had gained early control of the Lion's Peak pass against the desperate resistance of a handful of *requetés* and Falangists; but the overconfident leader of the Republican troops returned to Madrid, leaving a reduced force there. When on the 22nd Colonel Serrador's column arrived from Valladolid and attacked the remnant forces stationed at the Lion's Peak, the surprised and leaderless Republican force panicked and fled. Later the Nationalists had to face Republican reinforcements, including the all-Communist Thaelmann battalion; but in an overwhelming charge, on 25th July, Colonel García Escámez led his volunteers to victory and secured Somosierra Pass for the Nationalists. Onésimo Redondo and other Falangist comrades from Valladolid paid with their lives the victorious action. The Lion's Pass became known thereafter the Lions' Pass.

Oviedo: The great Spanish writer and humorist Enrique Jardiel Poncela describes well the liberation of Oviedo on 17th October 1936, as one of the main events determining the defeat of the Republic. After the initial defeat of the rebels in Madrid, Barcelona and Valencia, the Republican Government had almost everything in its favor to control the situation. The siege of the miners and troops which surrounded Oviedo from the very first days of the rising was broken by a Nationalist column, which had been capable of opening its way, against all odds, to the Asturian capital from Galicia. The reds made the same error as in Toledo, as they, obsessed with the idea of overwhelming General

Aranda, the defender of Oviedo, neglected what was evidently their best course of action: to make a concerted effort to stop the liberating column of Colonel Camilo Alonso Vega, advancing from Galicia and gaining ground centimeter by centimeter and responding to the dynamite cartridges of the miners with their hand bombs. The determination of those leading the miners was especially stubborn because their hate for Aranda was blinding them. Aranda was Republican, and they considered him a traitor, only because he loved Spain more than the Republic which was assassinating her. The heroism of the Oviedo's defenders and the courage of the Nationalist troops advancing towards the city under siege was ineffable, fighting all the time at a disadvantage of one to thirty. The corridor which united Galicia with Oviedo was kept for thirteen months! Aranda explained it this way:

> The advancing column was as thick as an arm at the point of departure, as thick as a wrist approaching Oviedo, only as thick as a stretched hand arriving to the city, but it still did not touch it, the hand then extended a finger... and through this finger the troops of Vega entered the city.

This explanation shows that Aranda was a man with talent, more talent than that of the leaders of the seventy five thousand encircling Oviedo during all the three months of siege. When the relieving force reached the embattled city, most of it was reduced to rubble. About half of Aranda's garrison was dead or wounded; but they had prevailed.

Not all heroic defenders in Asturias were as lucky as the defenders of Oviedo at that time. The defenders of the Simancas barracks in nearby Gijón were finally overwhelmed by the red militia...

But the defenders of Oviedo deserved their *Laureada de San Fernando* for posterity to remember.

Seville: General Queipo de Llano, who also had had Republican sympathies in the past, was assigned to lead the rising in Seville. He had just arrived in the city the day before and had just four officers with him. Before most of the military in the city had heard anything about the rising at the other side of the Gibraltar's strait, he moved quickly, and, in an astonishing demonstration of bluff and bravado, succeeded in taking the city for the Nationalists. According to Warren Carroll (*The Last Crusade*) his achievements would be incredible if they were not well documented.

Queipo set up his headquarters in an abandoned building. Then, he walked unannounced into the office of the General Villa Abrille, commander of the army in Andalucía and said: «I must tell you that the time has come to take a decision: either you are with me and my comrades or you are with this government which is leading Spain to its ruin». When General Villa Abrille did not respond immediately, Queipo declared him and his staff under arrest. He simply sent them into the next room, which had no lock, turned to a corporal standing by and ordered him to shoot anyone trying to leave. Apparently, nobody objected. Then he came back to the barracks and he found the commanding colonel and his men in military formation on the plaza. Queipo exclaimed «I congratulate you on upon your decision to side with your brothers-in-arms when the fate of our country is being decided!». When the colonel began to mumble that he had done no such a thing, Queipo relieved him from command and asked for volunteers to replace him. A young captain raised his hand. Queipo, then, told thereby the other officers that they were under arrest too. At about this time 25 Carlists, 15 Falangists and a few Civil Guards came in support of the rebel general. Later that day, he won over the commander of the artillery in Seville, brought his guns into Plaza San Fernando and opened fire on the building housing the civil government, which surrendered immediately. Workers in the city began building barricades. But that evening Queipo went on the radio. He proved a real master of radio propaganda, convincing listeners that he was in full command and would deal mercilessly with anyone resisting.

Queipo de Llano had much to answer for in his handling of events over the next six months as military governor for the Nationalists in the south. But had other local leaders of the rising shown half his bold panache, several hundreds of thousands of Spanish lives would have been saved.

CARDINAL GOMÁ AND THE BISHOPS'
COLLECTIVE LETTER

María Luisa Rodríguez Aisa, Professor of Political Sciences at the Universidad Complutense, Madrid, and very good friend of mine, is the author of a definitive book on the religious aspects of the Spanish Civil War: *El Cardenal Gomá y la Guerra de España: Aspectos de la gestión pública del Primado, 1936-1939* (CSIC: Madrid, 1981). Chapter 7 is devoted to the Collective Letter of the Spanish Bishops, 1st July 1937.

As it is well known, the Civil War had a tremendous International resonance. The Bishops' Collective Letter was signed almost unanimously by the Spanish Bishops (those who were still alive after the bloody persecution of the first six months of the war) with two exceptions. The Collective Letter was addressed to all the Bishops of the world with the object of explaining what was really going on in Spain, and how much was involved in the war for the future of Christian civilization under attack. The undersigned were 48, beginning with

1. Isidro Gomá y Tomás, Cardinal-Archbishop of Toledo.
2. Eustaquio Ilundáin y Esteban, Cardinal-Archbishop of Seville.
3. Prudencio Melo y Alcalde, Archbishop of Valencia.
4. Rigoberto Doménech Valls, Archbishop of Saragossa.
5. Manuel Castro Alonso, Archbishop of Burgos.
6. Agustín Parrado García, Archbishop of Granada.
7. Tomás Muñiz Pablos, Archbishop of Santiago de Compostela.
8. José Miralles, Archbishop-Bishop of Mallorca.

With 25 bishops and 5 *capitular* vicars following, the two exceptions were Cardinal Vidal i Barraquer, Archbishop of Tarragona, who had escaped miraculously to Rome in the first days of the war, and Bishop Mateo Mújica, Bishop of Álava, whose sympathies with the Basque Nationalists had made him *persona non grata* for the rebels who, in the first days of the war, and thanks to the Catholic *requetés*, had won Alava for the civic-military rising.

Cardinal Pacelli, then Secretary of State, on behalf of Pope Pius XI, had corresponded already in January 1937 with Cardinal Gomá, Archbishop of Toledo and Primate of Spain, saying that the Holy See was ready to send a pontifical letter to the separatist Basque priests, which were siding with the Popular Front, in order to mediate with Franco. It did not work. Then Gomá began consultations with all the Spanish bishops (many of whom had already issued pastoral letters justifying the civic-military rising) in order to explore the opportunity and the possible contents of a public pronouncement on the Spanish Civil War by all the bishops. Of special interest was also the correspondence between Gomá and Vidal i Barraquer, in which the latter made every effort to dissuade Gomá from such an initiative. Even Msgr. Mateo Mújica, from Rome, was at first favorable to Gomá's project. All the other bishops were fully committed in favor of the document.

In a second communication with Rome on the subject, Gomá makes it clear that Franco had complained to him that

the Catholic press in all the world, specially in Europe and particularly in France and Belgium...is totally at odds with the Episcopate [he meant the Spanish Episcopate]... in contrast with the true significance of the tremendous events which have occurred in Spain since last July.

Franco found it difficult to explain this behavior. According to Gomá, he suggested that the Spanish bishops publish a statement addressed to the bishops of all the world, requesting its reproduction in the Catholic press in order to put everything into a proper perspective. This would, surely, result in a patriotic clarification of the historical record, to the benefit of the Catholic cause.

Of course, Franco was fully convinced of the truth of his claims.

At a later time, one of the many jokes about Franco that circulated during the post-war period, was that, addressing the Sacred Heart, he said «Sacred Heart, have confidence in me», instead of saying the customary: «Sacred Heart, I have confidence in you».

The fact that the Collective Letter (CL) was written in response to previous statements in the opposite sense gives the document its outmost clarity. It is evident from the beginning that it aims at the legitimization of the movement of 18th July 1936, before world opinion. Given the prevailing circumstances, the Letter uses terms like *rising* or *civil-military movement*, not the word *crusade*, which was later to become common to describe the Spanish Civil War outside leftist circles. The Letter describes concrete facts and circumstances, but it maintains an attitude of understandable political independence, facing as it were an uncertain future. It points out vividly that Spain is suffering one of the greatest tribulations of her history. It may be noted also that many Catholic bishops in foreign countries, either collectively (Colombia, Mexico, Ireland, Paraguay, Peru, USA) or individually, had sent moral and financial support to their brothers in Spain.

It is noted in the CL itself that many foreign bishops were well aware that events in Spain transcended the significance of a purely local Civil War to become the expression of a *tremendous* commotion shaking the foundations of every day life in Spain and questioning the very existence of Spain as nation.

The Spanish bishops addressed therefore their brothers all over the world
... with the only purpose that truth shines forth, a truth (often) obscured by frivolity or malice, and (with the hope) that they help to spread it. It is a case of momentous gravity in which not only the political interests of a nation but the providential foundations of social life: religion, justice, authority and liberty, freedom of all citizens, are at stake. (*Por Dios y por España*: CL, 561).

The full text of the Collective Letter was published (as an *Appendix*) in *Por Dios y por España*, the writings of Cardinal Gomá during the war.

The Letter is divided as follows: 1. Motivation of this document. 2. Nature of the Letter. 3. Our stand before the war. 4. The five years preceding the war. 5. The military rising and the Communist revolution. 6. Character of the Communist revolution. 7. The National Movement. 8. Answered objections. 9. Conclusion.

The bishops make it clear that because the gravity of the facts transcended mere political disputations, it was incumbent on them to speak out as pastors in charge of the *true Magisterium*. They said they had a triple obligation: *of religion*, before so many testimonies and so grave aggressions; *of patriotism*, which they, as bishops, were the first to witness in defense of the good name of their country, Christianized by their predecessors; and *of humanity*, to prevent other nations from the ruinous devastation which had come from the bad example of following certain doctrines being used in Spain as a testing ground.

First, the Letter states categorically the non-belligerent position of the Spanish Bishops regarding the war. Since 1931 the Church had made efforts to collaborate for the common good «putting resolutely herself at the side of the *de facto* constituted powers». And, in spite of repeated affronts, she never had tried to alter national coexistence, but had tried to preserve and maintain it. The main reason of the Episcopal mission was always to advance peace, charity and pardon, proclaiming that

> ... with our best wishes for peace, we offer our generous pardon for those who are attacking us, and our charitable feelings for all. And over the battle fields we say to all our sons on both sides, the words of the Apostle: «The Lord knows how much do we love all in the heart of Jesus Christ» (CL, 564).

True peace —«tranquility in order, divine, national, social and individual»— had its own exigencies and, because of it, the war was the «ultimate remedy, a heroic remedy to put things back on the hinge of justice». The Collective Letter incorporated almost verbatim the affirmations on just war summarized in Cardinal Gomá's letter of January 1937.

> This is the standing of the Spanish Episcopate, the Spanish Church before the present war. She was persecuted and vexed before its breakout; she was the main victim of the fury of one of the contending factions; and she has not ceased to labor with its prayer, its exhortations and its influence to lessen the damages and to shorten the days of proof (CL, 565).

Second, the Collective Letter considered legitimate the rising because of the extreme danger to the very existence of Spain as a nation, due to the real menace of the Communist revolution. To the bishops, the war was brought up «by the temerity, the errors, the malice and the cowardice of those who could have avoided it governing to the nation according to justice».

The laws dictated from the advent of the Republic, because of their aggressive laicism, had created a climate of protest and rejection against the social authorities in a substantial part of the citizenry. Besides, the authorities had been overcome «on multiple and grave occasions» by anarchy. Events such as those that occurred in May 1931 (burning of churches); October 1934 (miners' revolution in Asturias), and February to July 1936 (unchecked increasing violence all over Spain) were a clear sign that public authorities had lost control, and were incapable of fulfilling their commitments. The democratic system was being adulterated, not because of its own mechanism, but because of the arbitrary exercise of the State's authority, and because of the coactive activities of the Government.

The bishops pointed out that the project of a Marxist revolution was already under way, and that «it would have exploded on the whole country if the civic-military movement had not stopped it». The revolution was, according to the CL, «ordered to the implantation of Communism» and consequently, to the liquidation of the Catholic Church, as one of its main objectives.

In other words, the true cause of the war was the disintegration of the religious, political and social order taking place during 1931-1936. The alternative was either to succumb to Communism or, in the last instance, to attempt to save the national identity and the foundations of the social order.

> ... It was in the national consciousness that, having exhausted all legal means, there was no other recourse than the force to keep order and peace; that powers alien to the authorities held to be legitimate had decided to subvert the established order and to violently implant Communism; and, because of the fatal logic of the facts, that there remained to Spain only one alternative: either to succumb before the definitive assault of destructive Communism, already planned and decided (as it occurred in those regions where the National movement had not succeeded) or to attempt, with titanic efforts, to get rid of the terrible enemy, saving the main principles of the social life with its national characteristics (CL, 569).

Confronting the civic-military movement were not only those forces loyal to the Republican Government but, specially, all the «forces of anarchy», the popular militias, increasingly controlled by Russia.

It may be noted however (and it is this author's personal opinion, quite apart from the considerations made in the Collective Letter), that the Spanish anarchists, no doubt guilty of many crimes and misdemeanors in the Civil War, must at least be credited with a brave and stubborn resistance to being fully controlled by Communism, already infiltrated in the Socialist Party. This should be counted as an important factor in the final outcome of the war, nearly lost at the beginning by the rebels, because of the overwhelming superiority in material means of the Government, as none other than Indalecio Prieto pointed out at the time.

Spain was divided into two fiercely contending opposite factions, which gave to the war the character of a national plebiscite. According to the Collective Letter:

> The civic-military rising was in its origin a national movement in defense of the fundamental principles of all civilized societies; in its further activity it has worked against that anarchy, allied with the forces at the service of a Government, which was unable to oversee the application of these [fundamental] principles (CL, 573).

The bishops conclude: 1st) «The Church, in spite of her peaceful spirit, and in spite of not willing the war, and of not having collaborated in it, could not be indifferent towards the fight». 2nd) The Church could not accept «behaviors, tendencies or intentions, in the present or in the future, that would denature the noble countenance of the National Movement in its origin...». 3rd) The Church affirms that «the civic-military rising had a double root in the popular consciousness: the patriotic [...] and the religious. The many Spanish martyrs, priests, religious and laymen must result in grave political responsibilities for those who would have the duty of reconstructing the State once peace is achieved.

The Collective Letter denied that the war was a conflict between Democracy and Statism. On the contrary, it said «rather than perishing completely at the hands of Communism [...], [the Church] is protected by a [Nationalist] leadership that, until now, has guaranteed the fundamental principles of every [civilized] society, irrespective of political tendencies».

In retrospect, it is not easy to do accurate quantitative estimates, but perhaps about thirty five percent of the Spanish population sided immediately with the rebels and about thirty five supported the Government, with the rest undecided or uncertain. The civic-military movement did rise in «defense of order, social peace and tradition...» while the Popular Front government was for «materialism, Marxism, communism and anarchism...», but it, immediately, could count on the overwhelming support of world opinion, deceived by an effective leftist propaganda. Those, fighting for God, country and freedom, may possibly have been less than their enemies, but, certainly, they fought with more determination, courage and discipline.

According to the Spanish bishops,

... the war was not undertaken to bring up an autocratic State over a humiliated nation, but it was undertaken to restore the national spirit with the vitality and the Christian freedom of the past. We are confident –said the bishops– that the [National] government would not accept foreign patterns to configure the future Spanish State.

The echo of the Collective Letter was great according to the report presented by Cardinal Gomá to the Metropolitan bishops.

Several editions were made to diffuse it throughout the world; one in Castilian; another in French; another in English, and, recently, another in Italian. The French, made upon request, reached 15,000 copies; the English distributed 6,000, and the Italian, 1,500. Besides, thanks to private initiatives, three editions in French have appeared in Belgium, one or two in Canada, and another one in France. From the US, new copies are needed, but it is known that one of the editions has reached 100,000 copies (August, 1937).

Among the many messages of solidarity, were two Collective Letters of the Irish and US bishops sent by the apostolic delegate A. G. Cicognani and of non-Catholic organizations, such as the Christian British Council, signed by H. W. Fox. The work of C. Bayle, *El mundo católico y la Carta Colectiva del Episcopado Español* (Burgos, 1938), lists in detail the resounding echoes of the Spanish Bishops' Collective Letter.

No doubt, Cardinal Gomá was a true Catalan and a model Spanish patriot who did much for his beloved Catalonia and his no less beloved Spain, as well as for the Catholic Church. Separatism in Catalonia, as much as in the Basque Provinces, has been always deleterious for the Catholic identity of these two Spanish territories.

GARCÍA LORCA AND MUÑOZ SECA

Federico García Lorca was certainly one of the greatest Spanish poets of the first half of the 20th century. Pedro Muñoz Seca, much less known internationally, was, no doubt, one of the most successful Spanish playwrights of the same period. There were many successful playwrights at that time in Spain, including Benavente, Arniches, Pemán, Jardiel Poncela, Mihura, etc. But no one's plays are so often performed nowadays again in Madrid as Muñoz Seca, specially his classic *La Venganza de Don Mendo*.

Both men died in 1936. García Lorca was assassinated in tragic circumstances in August; Muñoz Seca was assassinated with more than one hundred victims in November. At dawn 16th August, Lorca was arrested together with his brother-in-law Manuel Fernández Montesinos, a former Socialist Mayor of Granada. Lorca's brother-in-law was shot at dawn, along with 29 collaborators. By then, General Queipo de Llano's newly appointed governor of Granada, José Valdés, had shot a total of 236 less than a month from the rising (see Stanley G. Payne, *The Franco Regime, 1936-1975* [University of Wisconsin , Madison, 1987], p. 212). The following April, just a few months after being elected by his fellow generals Head of Government and Generalissimo, Franco dismissed Valdés because of the very high number of executions ordered by him in such a short time. García Lorca had been brought to Valdés' headquarters in Granada on the afternoon of the 16th, after being arrested in the home of Luis Rosales, a Falangist poet, who was a friend of Lorca. He had taken refuge there a few days before. It may be noted that, in spite of his leftist leanings, García Lorca was a self-confessed admirer of José Antonio Primo de Rivera, the Falangist leader condemned to death and shot in Alicante, a few months later. Queipo talked with Valdés on the phone on the 18th and told him to execute García Lorca, who was shot the very next day. It was certainly an indefensible decision, since García Lorca was never charged with any crime by any court. At that time, however, there was not yet a functioning Nationalist government. The very large number of crimes in the first weeks after the rising by the partisans of the Popular Front may explain but not justify García Lorca's assassination.

No less indefensible, of course, was the assassination of Pedro Muñoz Seca on 27th November 1936 in Paracuellos del Jarama, near Madrid. In the months preceding the tragic events of Paracuellos, many hundreds had been shot, as Cesar Vidal documents in *Paracuellos-Katyn: Un Ensayo Sobre el Genocidio de la Izquierda* (Libros Libres: Madrid, 2005); as well as before, in the last six months before the civic-military rising, and after 18th July 1936, in the Barracks of the Mountain, Madrid, near Plaza de España; and in the trains coming from Jaén, as well as in Ventas, Boadilla and Aravaca.

Félix Schlayer, dean of the consular representatives in Madrid, had been able to mobilize the diplomatic corps to provide refuge for many Madrilians, whose lives were in danger only because they did not approve of the way the Republican Government was handling the aggressive anarchy unleashed after February of 1936.

On 27th November, instructions from above came to the *checa* of San Antón, ordering the *release* of 113 prisoners, among them Pedro Muñoz Seca. They were brought to Paracuellos in buses driven by militia men (Communists) and shot collectively. It was rumored that when don Pedro was brought up to Paracuellos –great humorist as he was to the end–

he told his executioners: «There is one thing you cannot take away from me: my fear».

When the large number of assassinations of those days stopped temporarily, many thousands of Madrilians had been murdered fulfilling orders of the Republican Junta (Defense Board). The Council of Public Order was under the authority of the young Communist leader Santiago Carrillo. It may be noted that later it was an anarchist leader, Melchor Rodríguez, who authorized by García Oliver, the anarchist Minister of Justice in Valencia's government, put an end to the great number of killings of Paracuellos del Jarama.

Outside of Spain, the murder of García Lorca in 1936 is well known. But very few are aware of Muñoz Seca's murder the same year.

TESTAMENT OF JOSÉ ANTONIO PRIMO DE RIVERA

Testament which José Antonio Primo de Rivera and Sáenz de Heredia, thirty three years old, bachelor, lawyer, born and neighbor of Madrid, son of Miguel and Casilda (both resting in peace), words and grants in the Provincial Prison of Alicante, on the eighteenth of November of 1936:

Having been sentenced yesterday to death, I ask God, if He does not exempt me yet of that critical moment, that He keeps me till the end in the decorous conformity I have at present, and that when He judges my soul He does not apply the measure of my merits but the measure of his infinite mercy.

The scruple assaults me whether or not it is vanity or excessive attachment to the things of this earth, to give at this juncture an account of some of my deeds; but, on the other hand, I have drawn the faith of many of my comrades in a higher measure than that deserved by my merits (too well known to me to the point of saying this with frank and contrite sincerity), and taking into account that I have drown many of them to defy enormous risks and responsibilities, it would seem from my part unconsidered ingratitude to leave them with no explanation.

It is not necessary to repeat now again what so many times I have said and written about what the founders of *Falange Española* intended it to be. I am astonished that, even after three years, the great majority of our countrymen has persisted in judging us without beginning in the least to understand us, and without having looked for or accepted the minimum of information. If *Falange* consolidates itself into something durable, I hope everyone perceives the sorrow for so much blood spilled, having been unable to open a breach of serene attention in between the rage of one side and the antipathy of the other. May God forgive me for the part I might have had in provoking that spilled blood, and may the comrades who preceded me, receive me as the last one of them.

Yesterday, for the last time, I explained to the Court judging me what *Falange* is about. As on so many previous occasions, I reviewed and summarily put forward the old texts of our basic doctrine. Once more I detected in many faces, hostile at the beginning, first a light of surprise, then of sympathy. I think I read in their faces something like: «If we had known that, we would not be here!». And, certainly, neither would they be there then, nor would I be facing a popular Court, nor would others be killing each other all over Spain. It was not, however, a time for lamenting it, and I limited myself to defend the loyalty and courage of my comrades in order to win for them the respectful attention of their enemies.

That is what I was trying to do, I was not to trying win for me the posthumous false reputation of a hero. I did not make myself *responsible for everything*, neither did I adjust to any other variant of the romantic pattern. I defended myself with the best means at my disposal in my office as a lawyer, so dear to me and so diligently cultivated. Perhaps some future commentator may blame me for not having made a show. Let it be as it was. For me, leaving aside that I am not the first actor in what is happening, it would be monstrous and false to give away without a good defense a life which might still be useful, a life that God did not grant me to burn it out in holocaust to my vanity as in a fireworks. Also I did not descend to any dishonorable trick, nor did I endanger anybody with my defense, and I was cooperating, however, with the defense of my brothers Margot and Miguel, prosecuted with me and menaced with most grave penalties. But, because my duty as a lawyer counseled me not only certain omissions, but also certain charges based upon suspicions of having been brought on purpose in a territory kept submissive [to the Government], I should say now that these suspicions have not been confirmed and that they might have been produced by an exasperation and a loneliness, that now, facing my death, I cannot and should entertain any longer.

Another point remains for me to rectify. The isolation from all communication in which I have lived since very little after the present events began, was broken only by a North American journalist who, with the permission of the local authorities, asked me to give my testimony at the beginning of October. Until five or six days ago, when I come to read the indictment against me, I had no notice of the testimony attributed then to me, because neither the newspapers I had seen, nor any other available newspaper had reported that testimony. After reading it I affirm that, among the various statements to me attributed, unevenly faithful in reflecting my thoughts, there is one that I reject immediately: it is the one in which my comrades of the *Falange* are accused of cooperating with insurrectional side by side with «mercenaries brought from abroad». I have never said anything like that, and yesterday I said so before the Tribunal, even if so doing did not make me any favors. I should not insult this way military forces that have been protagonist in Africa of heroic services. And from here I cannot reproach my comrades when I don't know whether they are wisely or wrongly commanded, but I am sure they are trying to interpret the best they can, in spite of our lack of communications, my words and doctrines of always. May God grant that their warm candor is not abused in any other service than in that of the great Spain of which the *Falange* dreams.

May God grant that my blood be the last Spanish blood spilled out in civil discords. May God grant in peace to the Spanish people, so rich in heartfelt qualities, Fatherland, Bread and Justice.

Nothing else matters respecting my public life. As to my approaching death, I expect it, without boasting (because never is it pleasant to die at my age) but without protest. May God accept as a sacrifice to compensate in part for what of selfishness and vanity might have been in much of my life. I forgive with all my soul all who might have harmed or offended me, with no exception, and I beg the pardon for any offense, great or little. Having said that, I proceed to declare my last will in the following

CLAUSES

First: I wish to be buried, in conformity with the rites of the Catholic, Apostolic, Roman religion, which I profess, in blessed ground, under the protection of the Holy Cross.

Second: I make heirs of mine by equal parts to my four brothers Miguel, Carmen, Pilar and Fernando Primo de Rivera y Sáenz de Heredia, with the right to increase his or her part among them if any of them die before me with no descendants. If there were descendents, the corresponding part of my dead brother should go to the descendents by equal parts. This disposition is valid even if the death of my brother has taken place before I grant this testament.

Third: I do not make any legacy neither do I impose on my heirs any effective legal obligation; but I beg from them:

A)   That they take care with my goods to ensure the well being and benefit of our aunt María Jesús Primo de Rivera y Orbaneja, whose maternal abnegation and tender integrity in the twenty seven years in charge of us we could not pay with treasures of gratitude.

B)   That, in my memory, some goods of mine and some everyday souvenirs be given to my official colleagues, specially to Rafael Garcerán, Andrés de la Cuerda and Manuel Sarrión, so loyal for years and years, so efficient and so patient with my not very comfortable company. To them and to all the rest I give my thanks and I ask them to remember me with not too much annoyance.

C)   That they distribute my personal things among my best friends, well known to them, and very specially among those who for longer time and more closely have shared with me the joys and adversities of our *Falange Española*. They and the rest of our comrades occupy at present in my heart a fraternal place.

D)   That they reward the oldest servants in our house, to whom I am grateful for their loyalty and to whom I beg pardon for any inconvenience due to me.

Fourth: I name legal administrators accountants and distributors of this heritage, jointly, for a term of three years, and with the usual higher attributions, to my very close lifelong friends Raimundo

Fernández Cuesta y Merelo and Ramón Serrano Súñer, to whom I beg specially:

A)   That they review my private papers and destroy all of a very personal character, those which involve purely literary work, and those which are simple outlines and projects in an early state of elaboration, as well as any works forbidden by the Church or of pernicious reading that may remain among my papers.

B)   That they collect all my discourses, articles, circular letters, prologues of books, etc., not to publish them –except if they consider it indispensable– but to serve as pieces of justification whenever it is discussed the present Spanish period of politics in which my comrades and I have intervened.

C)   That they take care of my urgent substitution in handling the professional matters entrusted to me, with the help of Garcerán, Sarrión and Matilla, and to get paid some minutes due to me.

D)   That with the highest possible urgency and effectiveness they bring forth the solemn rectifications to the offended persons and entities referred to in the introduction of this testament.

For which, I thank them now cordially. And in those terms I leave ordered my testament in Alicante the said day, eighteen of November of 1936, at five in the afternoon, in three other sheets of paper, besides this one, all of them numbered, dated and signed in its margin.

* * *

José Antonio's testament shows very clearly that he may have been (and in fact he was) a very harsh critic of Rousseaunian liberalism, but it shows also that it would be quite wrong to class him as a *fascist*.

Hitler's Nazism and Mussolini's Fascism (this last to a lesser extent) were pagan totalitarian movements, with much in common with Stalin's Communism. *Falange Española*, on the other hand, was from the very beginning an authoritarian, but deeply Catholic, movement. Fiercely anti-Communist, sympathetic to some extent with anarchism (of course, only to a some extent), strongly patriotic, and therefore firmly opposed to any separatism, *Falange* was very much in favor of worker's rights, and very much hostile to the abuses of plutocratic capitalism. In principle, *Falange* was not opposed to representative government, from municipal government to the highest spheres of government.

Of course, it should be noted that José Antonio was a poet rather than an academic political scientist, but his *Falange*, and the *Falange* envisaged by his close friends and collaborators (like Onésimo Redondo, Ruiz de Alda, Fernández Cuesta and even Serrano Súñer, to name a few) had more in common with what was known in the first half of the 20th century as State Corporatism than with any kind of Fascism.

In summary, José Antonio's doctrine, which defined man as «portador de valores eternos» (carrier of *eternal values*, in other words an *immortal soul*), could use the term *totalitarian* only in a broad Catholic sense necessarily compatible in any case with individual freedom. For him, the political parties were *not* the only potential channels of ordered democratic representation. But he was certainly no *fascist*.

GARCÍA MORENTE'S *EXTRAORDINARY EVENT*

Manuel García Morente was a certainly one of the intellectual stars of the Spanish University in the first half of the 20th century. Born in Arjonilla, Jaén, in 1886, very young, he had won in 1922, which still relatively young, the chair of Ethics, at the Central University, Madrid. A very distinguished colleague of men like Ortega y Gasset, Zubiri, Besteiro… he had an enormous influence on successive generations of students. He became Dean of the Faculty of Philosophy and Letters in 1931. At the time, he was a convinced disciple of Immanuel Kant, and he was moderately inclined to the Left, as a protégé of the *Institución Libre de Enseñanza*. His excellent translation of Spengler's *Decline of the West* (2 vol. 1918-22) was widely acclaimed. Some of his students (including my mother) found his lectures more interesting and stimulating than those of his most famous colleagues at the time.

On the night from the 29th to the 30th of April, 1937, after listening on the radio to Berlioz's *The Infancy of Jesus*, he experienced what he termed an *extraordinary event*, which determined his conversion to Catholicism, and, later, being a widower, and father of two girls, his decision to become a Catholic priest. He was ordained in 1940, and, after a short, but intense apostolic life in post-war Spain, he died prematurely in Madrid, in December 1942.

In the following, the reader will find a summary of Morente's account of the extraordinary event, written to explain it to don José María García Lahiguera, director of the Seminary of Madrid (whose process of beatification-canonization is presently under way), who was then Morente's spiritual director.

* * *

Assassination of his son-in-law

The event took place in the night from the 29th to the 30th of April 1937, approximately at two am. Let me put forward a few minor antecedents, necessary, very convenient to know, before beginning with the full account.

On 28th August 1936 my son-in-law was assassinated in Toledo. I had for him a great affection, mixed with something like respect and admiration. He was a young man, twenty nine years old, deserving to be loved in every respect; his moral behavior had always been exemplary. I don't think I am mistaken if I say that he arrived at his matrimony in a state of perfect purity. His personal life had been one of a religiosity without blemish. He was a member of *Nocturnal Adoration*. Perhaps this circumstance was not alien to his tragic death. All in all, his character was joyful, optimistic, youthful and even boyish in certain respects. He loved mathematics –in which he was very well versed– and sports. His physical appearance was rather pleasant. He was what one may class as a handsome young man. In his career of Engineering he was facing a brilliant future. No doubt he would have been able to achieve an excellent position. I was really charmed with him. He had given me a very beautiful little granddaughter, and shortly –two months– before his death, was born the grandson. I was notified of his death in the University, at the event of transferring formally the deanship –deprived of it by the red Government– to my successor, Mr. Besteiro. From my home, they told me, by phone, about the death of my son-in-law. The impression it produced on me was such that I fell down dizzy to the floor. When I recovered my senses, I asked Mr. Besteiro to use all of his influence to bring my daughter and the children from Toledo to Madrid.

In effect, Mr. Besteiro, I should say, very nobly, obtained an official car with two guardsmen to pick up my daughter and her children. Two days later, at eleven at the night, they arrived in Madrid. We, at home, had been waiting for them since eight o'clock. Those were three hours of great anguish. Tragic scenes crossed my mind all the time. I imagined my daughter assassinated, my grandchildren taken away by hostile or indifferent hands and brought up to who knows what infantile camp or asylum, lost for ever. The anguish kept all of us nervous and expectant at home. At last, the car arrived, at eleven in the night, and with it my daughter, the children and two servants, in good health all of them.

If I tell you all these details it is because I think they are useful in understand the state of mind that was taking hold of me. My sensibility, itself excitable, was becoming increasingly exacerbated. The tragedy of my poor daughter, widow at twenty one, with two children after two years of marriage, upset completely my thinking, my feelings, my entire life. On my shoulders were falling back again all the heavy responsibilities of a father. And at such times! When the life, the property, the reputation, utterly defenseless, were at the mercy of any wicked man willing to trample on them. A tragic silence prevailed in my home, full of anguish and terror. I did not go outside at all. Nobody went out, except the indispensable for the ordinary needs of life.

One day, militia-men came to take away the eldest son of our neighbors living in the same floor. The poor boy was taken to jail and later assassinated at Paracuellos. Another day, we burned systematically in the heating boiler all the documents and the correspondence I kept since the year I was Sub-Secretary of Public Instruction in the Government of General Berenguer. The following day –it was providential– they came up to inspect my home. We spent the whole day watching behind the venetian blinds of the windows all the cars stopping at the door of our home. With our heart shrinking we counted the steps of the assassins going up, and, when they passed our storey, we all let out a sigh of relief. Death was coming to another home! My daughters, my sisters-in-law, my aunt, the nanny we had with us for twenty six years, all joined together in a corner of the house and spent there hours and hours praying. I could not, and perhaps did not then know how to pray. But I don't know what interior force pushed me to approve and to be grateful for that tender and submissive faith of the good women.

In that situation, on 26th September, scarcely one month after the assassination of my son-in-law, I received early in the morning the confidential warning that I should urgently leave the home and get out of Spain, right away if possible, since some elements, discontent with my performance as dean of the Faculty of Philosophy and Letters, had decided upon my death, as it was usual then. I obeyed prudently that advice and counsel. I was able to obtain a safe-conduct through a minister who was a friend of mine, and with the still valid passport with which I had gone to Poitiers in the first days of July, I left for Barcelona and for France. In Barcelona I had some scary moments. Having been taken for another person, I was almost on the verge of been detained. At last, I got out of Spain and I arrived in Paris on 2nd October. I had seventy five francs in my pocket.

I repeat that, even at the risk of boring you with insignificant details, that it is necessary to relate all antecedents which might perhaps contribute to make plausible a natural explanation of that event which to me seems supernatural. Because you must have with you all the data useful to judge over the case, and the most important datum is the state of mind in which, little by little, the train of events was submerging me. I firmly believe that this state of mind is insufficient to account fully for certain aspects and subtleties of what happened, but I must tell you fully everything, so that you can judge with entire knowledge.

I arrived, thus, in Paris without money and with my soul full of anguish and pain, corroded by moral preoccupations. Had I done right in abandoning my home and my daughters, and putting myself selfishly out of danger? On the other hand, if the confidence received was true –and I had no motive to doubt it, and I had many reasons to give it credit, since the person who transmitted it to me was absolutely faithful and deserving of confidence–, I would have been assassinated already or, at least, imprisoned, and therefore prevented from helping my people, and perhaps even endangering them more than would have happened if they had exiled me in Paris. Between these two ideas oscillated my conscience, which sometimes accused me of being a fugitive, selfish and coward, and on other occasions absolved me, and commended me as prudent and cautious. Even today, when the facts have been demonstrated with more than sufficient evidence that I was right in leaving Madrid, I still find out in some inner corner of my soul certain reproaches of being cowardly and selfish when I recall my behavior at that time, getting out precipitously from Madrid. What do you think?

In Paris, God shielded me enough, saving me from total misery, and however, not enough to erase from my soul that humiliation, anguish and grief. A very good friend of mine, a Spaniard who had, and still has, a small flat in Paris, put at my disposal a room with a bed and a wardrobe. An excellent lady, French, widow of an old schoolfellow at the Sorbonne –dead gloriously for his country in 1914– charitably invited me to come to her dining room. In the house of my friend don Ezequiel Selgas, I spent the nights and the mornings. I went for lunch and dinner to Madame Malovoy. But, since Mr. Selgas, acting as secret courier from Paris to Biarritz (between don José Quiñones de León and the count of the Andes), was days and nights away from Paris, for me it was the case frequently to be alone in my friend's flat entire days and nights. Here is another small detail, but perhaps important. Because that loneliness, specially at night, could have influenced greatly my state of mind.

I suffer from insomnia a good deal. In normal times I usually combat the lack of sleep by means of psychological tricks that my experience has shown me to be effective: for example, to review in my mind philosophic theories, or physical, or mathematical theories, or chess problems –I was very fond of this game in my first youth, achieving results well above average–; in summary, to review a series of complicated ideas in all of which I had no personal or affective interest at all. But all these methods which I use successfully to reconcile sleep fail utterly when I have in my soul a profound, persistent emotion, because it is evident that I cannot benefit from them if my imagination flies after the sentimental, affective preoccupation which is obsessing me. Due to that, when I am truly under the heavy weight of a profound preoccupation, the insomnia is almost invincible, and only physical fatigue, at high hours in the morning, and only for a short time, is able to make me sleep.

Well, in Paris, the insomnia was the almost normal state of my very bad nights. I spent them questioning myself round and round whether I had acted right or wrong when I left my daughters to come to Paris, and on how I could manage to earn money, and on how to get out of my humiliating situation, and on how to bring out of Spain my daughters and my family, and on how to care for their subsistence away from my country (I, who was myself, then, living from the charity of others) in case I were able to bring them out of Spain. Also, I sometimes reviewed in my memory the whole course of my life: I saw how baseless was that comfortable satisfaction about myself in which I had been living; I perceived painfully the incurable spiritual restlessness which was growing within me, day by day.

Often I had to jump out of my bed, incapable of suffering any longer the insomnia, to walk up and down feverishly, then taking a book, which would fall very soon from my hands. What gave me more consolation was to open the window, and in spite of the cold weather, to remain for hours contemplating –it was the last eight floor– the immensity of Paris, and, in the background, the massive Montmartre and the light of the Eiffel Tower.

I began attempts, random attempts, to bring out my daughters from Spain through the British Embassy. They failed. I began then other attempts through the International Red Cross. I have had no answer as yet. And, curiously, these failures did not impress me too much, because the infinite longing of seeing them was considerably tempered by two considerations: first, that I was receiving regular letters from Madrid –through an interposed third person– , letters which assured me of their good health and their financial status. I had left with them a not negligible sum of money; and second, that, given the absolute penury which I was suffering, the perspective of having to cope, without a cent, for the needs of three persons in Paris, terrified me.

Then, at the end of January, 1936, a coup of good luck modified somewhat my position. I received a letter from the Garnier Frères Editors asking me to come to their offices. Full of curiosity and suspecting something favorable, I came to the Garnier's office. As a matter of fact, Mr. Garnier made me the proposition of making a new dictionary, French-Spanish and Spanish-French, in substitution for the old one, and out of print Salvá, made up many years before. A friend of mine, a Catalan editor, who, like me, and many others, had escaped to Paris, had spoken to Garnier about me as a person capable of taking care of the work in question. I accepted the proposal and the conditions asking to be paid monthly for my monthly deliveries of the original. I set myself to work feverishly. And I felt much better and much more consoled. I had, at least, a diurnal antidote, something with which to fill up the day's hours. The nights, unfortunately, could not be subtracted so easily from the claws of insomnia and from the worries, uneasiness and moral and spiritual anxieties. At the end of February I had the great satisfaction of collecting one thousand francs as a result of my work, and I ran to compensate, as well as I could, the lady who so generously was letting me eat each day at her home. It was not too much, but it was sufficient to lessen a little the cruel and humiliating feeling in which I was living since five months earlier.

Fifteen days later, in other words in mid-March, another *coup de théâtre*. I received a cable from Buenos Aires, signed by my old professor Alberini, dean of the Faculty of Philosophy and Letters of Buenos Aires, offering me the chair of Philosophy at the University of Tucumán (Argentina). Reply paid. I pondered for five minutes and answered right away with my acceptance, but under the condition that my daughters and grandchildren were able to get out of Spain to accompany me. Convinced that the response was going to be affirmative, I devoted myself feverishly to the task –now with all my soul– of looking for a way of bringing my family out of Spain. What to do? How to achieve such a difficult task? At that time, mid-March 1937, there were days at which I was three nights in a row without a sleep and unable to do anything as a result of the cruel insomnia; at most, I could manage half an hour or one hour of sleep in the late morning. No matter how much I thought about it, I was unable to focus on the problem of how to get my daughters out of Spain. How? Just then, when the Argentine offer could solve the problem of feeding my family out of Spain; just then, I did not see any light, any opening to go through.

Desperate, there were moments at which, exacerbated again by the painful moral scruple of having abandoned my family in Madrid, the idea assailed me –very strange in me, who was not a believer– that the contradiction between the actual possibility of taking care of the needs of my family away from Spain and the impossibility of arriving at a way to get them out together was God's punishment for my selfishness and cowardice. The first time the idea of God's punishment crossed my mind, it was something fleeting and transitory, in which I did not stop to ponder. But, at night, the same idea resurfaced again, and this time with such a clarity and persistence, that I had to pay it greater attention. But it was only to look at it, so to say, contemptuously and to reject it with annoyance, with intellectual pride, with human arrogance: «Don't be silly» I said to myself. And my train of thought cast over this poor little idea, humble and good, such a pile of philosophical, scientific representations, etc... that they drowned it in its infancy.

A few hours later something occurred to me which was at least strange. I was visiting frequently the house where lived, in Auteuil, don José Ortega y Gasset. To go there I had to pick up the Metro and I had to get out at the Avenue Mozart station, from which, on foot, I went through the street of l'Assomption up to the house of my good friend. I had never paid any attention to the name of that street nor to the reason for that name. But that day, somehow, coming out of the Metro stairway to Avenue Mozart, it struck me with the memory of my very dear wife (dead some years before, N.T.) at the same moment at which, lifting my head, my eyes became fixed on a little plaque saying «Rue de l'Assomption». Happy memories crowded my mind at that moment. «This street –I thought– is called street of the Assumption because, no doubt, it is where there was the convent of the Assumption, a convent of the same religious order as the one at which my wife was educated in Málaga. It is very clear! The mother house was established in Auteuil. And in Auteuil I am. Therefore in this area there must be the primitive convent of the nuns who so well educated my good wife and my daughters. Let us see». And walking slowly I looked carefully at all the buildings in my path. It did not take me too long to discover the convent. There it is still. A garden with very old trees makes up what survives of the immense park converted now into houses for rent. For a long time I examined the main facade of the convent, at present a house of retreat and rest for ladies and sick mothers. The street which next to the convent today is called «Rue Meillert de Brou», which is the maiden name of María Eugenia, the foundress of the Assumption order. Many times I had I gone nearby in those days and those months, and never had I seen anything about the street or the convent or any other thing related to them.

I arrived pensive and preoccupied to the house of don José Ortega y Gasset. And there and then I met in the hall a professor from Madrid, visiting don José, whom I knew very well and with whom I had a close and affectionate relationship. This gentleman was not, and is not *red*, but he had the misfortune of having his sons –all of them male and already grown up– divided on the Spanish question. One of them was serving as first Lieutenant of Engineering (volunteer) in Franco's army. The other, however, a physician, was the personal secretary of doctor Negrín. In the conversation came up the proposition I had received of a chair in Argentina, my response, and the very urgent need I had of getting my family out of Spain to bring them with me to America. Then, that gentleman said that his son, personal secretary of Dr. Negrín, was coming from Valencia the following day, and that he would talk to him of my wish, and that he would get me an interview with him, who perhaps could do something.

Providential coincidences

I was astonished. The combination of things which were happening to me had truly an extraordinary and incomprehensible character. Around me, or better, over me and independently of me, something was interlacing, *without any minimal intervention on my part*, all my life. The phone call of Garnier, the entrusting to me of the dictionary, the offer of a chair in Argentina, this very happy encounter with the father of the personal secretary of Negrín, nothing of it had been worked out, nor procured, nor suspected by me. I remained completely passive and ignorant of *everything which was happening to me*. It could be said that some unknown power, absolute master of all, was fixing, without me, everything mine. More, everything I had done or attempted by my own initiative had gone wrong, or had failed; my dealings with the British Embassy, with the International Red Cross, all my efforts to find work in Paris, everything had failed miserably. On the contrary, events that I could not even imagine were falling upon me as rain from heaven, events in which I had had no part at all. I had the impression of being a miserable little bit of straw pushed by an all-powerful hurricane.

For a third time, the idea of *Providence* was pinned down in my mind. For a third time, however, I rejected it with stubborn pride. But also with a certain vague feeling of anguish and confusion. It was too evident that I alone, by myself, could do nothing, and that everything, good or bad, that was happening to me had its source and origin in another power very different and highly superior. Still, I did take refuge in the cosmic idea of universal determinism, and when for a moment I entertained the idea of *asking*, asking to God, in other words, of praying –which was, no doubt, the most logical idea and the most congruent with everything which was taking place–, I rejected it also as stupid puerility. How crazy!

I had, in fact, an interview with the son of the professor, who arrived to Paris from Valencia by plane, the following day. I explained to him my wish. I told him that Negrín knew me well. I begged him to do his best to get my daughters and grandchildren out of Spain. Negrín was not at the time president of the Council of Government, but Finance Minister within the Government of Largo Caballero. The professor's son promised me to do anything in his power to satisfy my wishes. I came out well impressed, and full of optimism and hope. I wrote to my daughters a very well pondered letter.

Many times I had said them that they should not move, for anything in the world, out of Madrid, in one of those more or less forced expeditions to Valencia. It worried me deeply the mere idea of those roads bombed, those forced evacuations by truck, among militia men and women, at the risk of any fatal encounter. But I had to tell them now that their exit was my thing, under my advice and doing exactly everything I ordered them, following the instructions of the professor's son. The letter, therefore, was delicate and difficult. Thanks God, they understood it perfectly.

And, as a matter of fact, on 2nd April, I received a telegram from Valencia announcing their arrival in the Mediterranean capital. Two days after, I received a letter in which I was told that the travel from Madrid to Valencia had taken place happily by car, telling me about the interview with Negrín, who had received them very kindly and promised to get the necessary passport for Paris in a short time. I was swimming in joy. It seemed to me that in a few days I was to have the happiness of embracing them. I had already arranged for their lodging. An old friend of mine, fellow at the Sorbonne and professor at the University of Caen, had put at my disposal the flat he had in Paris, which he used only in vacation time.

I waited impatient the telegram confirming the day and the time of their arrival. Three days were gone by. «There must be –I thought– bureaucratic difficulties». As a matter of fact, my daughters said that bureaucratic problems were obstructing the matter, but that they had the word of the Minister of the Interior to get the passport the following day. A slight uneasiness, a kind of dark presentment rising in my soul was rapidly suppressed by cold reasoning. No, I should not be afraid; they had promised to give them the passport, therefore they were ready to give them; it must be a matter of days. I calmed down myself and as usual tried to put again my confidence in the regularity of human mechanisms. But three more days went by without receiving the telegram longed for. I was beginning to get restless again. And again I received letter from Valencia and again my daughters assured me that they had the firm promise of receiving the passport, that there was a jam at the Government offices and that I should be patient, etc., etc… Reading this letter, my heart was again bitten by doubts, by apprehensions and grief. What will happen? Would it be possible that in Valencia they were mocking them with vain promises?

Confidence in the natural determination of causes and effects collapsed again in my soul, and a deep anxiety got hold of me again. I could do nothing. Whatever had to happen far from me, had to happen with no chance of any effective action from my part. Alone in Paris, from the eighth floor of the home in Boulevard Sérurier, I was condemned to wait, in anguish, the exploding of events which were arranging or disarranging themselves on top of my head. Those nights were atrocious nights. «What are you doing with me –I thought–, God, Providence, Nature, Cosmos, whatever you are?». My impotence, my ignorance, a gloomy night awaiting me, and nothing, nothing absolutely, awaiting only the decision of events to come. To wait! And how to wait without knowing what? What kind of hope is that hope which does not know what to hope? A hope which does not what to hope is properly... despair. A strange feeling began to take hold of me, a kind of total, absolute desperation, a desperation of my whole being, an infinite laziness from which I got away only as under a strong whip, precipitating myself into a feverish and overexcited state of mind.

Four or five days passed without any news. My anxiety, my grief seemed to be reaching paroxysm. Some times I felt like a fool, literally absent, unable to think of anything. Other times I got out to the street and walked till fatigue made me stop. But that was even worse, because I came home so tired that it became impossible to sleep. At most, a kind of drowsiness got hold of me, but it was an uneasy sleep which did not do me any good.

Towards 20th April, I received another letter from Valencia which said, half in disguise, that there were *some difficulties for the projected trip*. This news, which confirmed my suppositions, did not add anything to what was waking already in my soul. But, of course, it intensified the depressive state in which I found myself. The most distinctive feature, perhaps, of this state was the feeling of *absolute impotency*, total passivity, of having no part on the gears moving my life, and in front of it, my pride rose so furious that I was unable to accept seeing myself reduced to so *absolute impotency*. This internal contradiction between the impotent will with full effective volitions, and the implacable (albeit *de incognito*) development of the events; this abyss between a self who wills to be and a reality which is what is, independent of the willing self, was what tortured me unspeakably.

Another week came by this way without news from Valencia. On 27th April I received a telegram saying: «Impossible to travel. Tell us whether to come back to Madrid or go to Barcelona». My suspicions were materializing. The Government denied exit to my daughters. Because it was feared, it was taken for granted, but it produced in me a tremendous impact.

First, it produced in me true rage and indignation against the red government. I gave then free inner rein to my insults. There was no doubt for me that the reds were keeping my family as hostages to keep me silent and inactive. I did answer the telegram counseling them to move to Barcelona, where we had very close and dear relatives in whose company, I thought, my daughters would survive better the moral as well as the material situation.

Immediately, a great depression, physical and intellectual, got hold of me. For some hours I was silly, indifferent, totally incapable of thinking about what was happening to me. I remember well that for a long while I lay in bed, following distracted the back and forth of a fly (or whatever) on the ceiling and on the wall next to it. Slowly the contours of the situation began to look clear to me. My hopes were all going down. I would have to be forced to renounce the chair in America, to renounce my daughters and my grandchildren, and forced to continue in Paris my life of insomnia and continuous preoccupations. No doubt, I would earn with the dictionary enough to pay for my own expenses. But, persuaded as I was that the war was going to be long, I saw the future to be extremely dark. And my daughters? Perhaps they were better off in Barcelona than in Madrid, in the company of excellent relatives and better protected. But, till when? Because now, the Government having denied them their exit, it would be useless to try it by other means, since it seemed clear to me that the Government *was unwilling* to let them getting leave Spain. What fortune would be waiting for them in the future?

The whole day of the 27th and the whole night there was revolving around in my head the same thoughts: *my* situation, *my* daughters, *my* house in Madrid, *my* immediate and remote future, the future of *my* people. On the 28th my friend Selgas left for Biarritz, and I was alone for some days. I decided, so to say, to relish that solitude. (Let me tell you that I never was afraid of being alone: to the contrary, I always enjoyed it very much; several times I have written in praise of it and I try to enjoy it as often as possible with considerable pleasure, and today, now, I long for it). I phoned Madame Malovoy to tell her that I would not come for lunch and dinner for several days, and, with a certain intimate pleasure, I walked back and forth in the flat to convince myself –childish occurrence– that I was alone.

Right away, the idea came to me that it was foolish to give the imagination free rein to go round and round aimlessly without any order, letting it follow freely the natural psychological association of ideas. It was therefore necessary to think orderly and methodically, not at the whim of my capricious imagination. Otherwise I was in a grave danger of falling –who knows?– into veritable mental perturbation. So, I began to make a general review of all that had happened to me since the war began and of the most important things I had pondered since then. The result evidently was: since the beginning of the war I had not intervened at all in my own life, or in the real context of the events in my own existence. My life, the events of my life, had taken place without me, without my intervention. In some sense, it could be said that I had witnessed them, but I had not caused them in anyway. Who was, or what was the cause of that life which, being mine, was not mine? Because the curious and strange thing was that all these events were events of my life, therefore, mine; but, on the other hand, they had not been caused or provoked not even suspected by me; in other words, they were not mine. There was here an evident contradiction. On the one hand, my life belongs to me, because it makes up the real historical content of my being in time. But, on the other hand, that same life does not belong to me, it is not, strictly speaking, mine, since its contents are in every case, produced and caused by something alien to my will.

I found but one solution to this antinomy: something or somebody different from me makes my life and delivers it to me, ascribes it to my individual being. That something or somebody, different from me, who makes my life, may explain sufficiently why my life, in a certain sense, is not mine. But that this life, made by the other, is given as a gift to me to be attributed to me, explains, in a certain sense, that I do not consider it as mine. Only in this way is it possible to resolve the contradiction or opposition between the perception that that life is not mine, because another did it, and, that, however, it is mine, because I alone live it.

But, arriving at this conclusion, two new problems came up: First, who is that something which makes up my life in me and then gives it to me? Second, what if I do not accept the gift? If I don't want that life which I have not made myself? Is this a free act properly mine, or it is a metaphysical necessity? Confronting the gravity of these two questions I remained perplexed and disconcerted.

(It seems to me, don José María, that I am abusing your patience and your goodness. Am I abusing them indeed? I hope your patience and goodness are so great that you continue reading. If they are not, please stop reading and tear to pieces these sheets of paper. I should say that, for my part, I cannot stop and shorten it more than what the gravity of the matter allows me).

A kind of spiritual tranquility came then over my soul, because I noticed, with great joy, that my preoccupations had gone suddenly from the domain of the particular and selfish into the domain of the general, the universal if you wish, the metaphysical. In fact, I was not thinking particularly of myself, but of human life, in general, through the windows of my particular case. This, I insist, made me glad, because that attitude of egoism and solipsism has been always a little repugnant to me, and also because I think it is not a good method of solving problems –even the most personal and intimate problems– to look at them from an exclusively subjective point of view. Truth, even individual truth, is always, in some respect, objective and general truth, and if this objective and general aspect is lost, it becomes very likely that the individual and personal decisions fail utterly. I decided therefore myself to embark upon a methodical investigation of the two problems which I had just formulated to myself.

I began, in a orderly manner, tackling the first. Who is this something different to myself who makes my life and gives it to me? There came clearly and immediately to my mind the idea of God. But this caused to appear on my lips immediately an ironic smile, a smile of ironic pride. «Come on –I thought–, God, if there is one, does not care about anything but about his own being. Let us forget about puerilities». And, indeed, I made an internal act of rejection of those, so called, puerilities. But to my surprise, those puerilities insisted in not going away. And then something stupendous happened, incomprehensible to me, unless by the evident help of grace; and it was that, without my noticing it at first, I began to proceed with a method strictly opposite to the one I generally used when dealing with these matters.

In general, when facing a philosophical or metaphysical problem, I proceed in my intimate investigation by embracing affectionately the thesis which fits and satisfies me better; and only thereafter by putting the pertinent objections, which then I try to solve, counter, and destroy, always with the intimate hope that, before my rational conscience, there prevails at the end the first thesis, the one embraced by me. When, on occasions, those difficulties with which I attack dialectically my initially preferred thesis become strong and decisive, and are finally up to destroying it, I become utterly disheartened, and it becomes very hard for me to distance myself from that which I see as erroneous, and to embrace –painfully– that which I see as truthful. Till, after some time, I give, at last, my heart to the thesis which is evidently true, and then I would equally find it thereafter painful to disregard it.

Well, this is what was most extraordinary in what then happened: that, during the internal debate with myself, all my affection went in favor, not of the anti-providentialist thesis which I had taken as the departing point, but in favor of the providentialist objections that I had been forced to oppose to the original thesis. Summing up, obedient as I was (due to my inertia due to my past) to the command that my intellectual pride was dictating to me against those *puerilities*, I began, in fact, my internal debate putting forward as starting point the thesis of natural determinism by means of causes and effects, in other words, by efficient causes: but very soon I noticed that –and this is the stupendous and the extraordinary– my heart was not with the thesis, but with the objections, and that those *puerilities* pleased me more than the supposed wisdom of strict causal determinism. Each time I discovered or remembered an argument against that natural determinism my heart gladdened, thus showing that I was, evidently, with the objections, and therefore against the thesis.

One objection, above anything else, made me full of joy: that this life which is mine but I do not make, only receive, is made up of events *full of meaning*. Now, a mere natural determinism –physical, historical, psychological– can produce events, but not events *full of meaning*, not those elements, as life events are, which are intelligible and intelligent, ordered wisely to certain ends and to certain effects. It would be very time consuming –and it is not necessary– to develop all of this properly. It may suffice to say that when night was approaching, a little crisis had taken place in my operative intellectual device. On the one hand, the idea of divine Providence, which makes our life and gives it to us, was already deeply engraved in my spirit. On the other hand, I could not conceive that Providence in not other way than as a supremely intelligent, supremely active, source of life, my life and all other lives; in other words, as a full complex or system of facts *full of sense*.

Arriving at this conclusion, I experienced a great consolation. I was stunned at it. How is it possible –I thought– that the idea of that wise, powerful, active and orderly Providence, which had just dealt me such a tremendous blow, could now give me consolation? I did not understand anything, but the fact was utterly evident. The fact was that I felt much more tranquil, serene and peaceful. (Much later, reading Saint Augustine, I discovered the real key to this enigma in his words: «Restless is my heart till it rests in You»). At that moment, I was unable to give another explanation, but the common and psychological: that the soul seized by anguish, impotence and ignorance begins to console itself with the idea that there is a reason, a cause, even if it does not know *what is* this cause or reason. The one thought that there was a wise Providence was enough to give me peace; even if I did not see the reason or cause of the cruelty that that Providence was inflicting on me by the denial of the return of my daughters.

The night of the 28th to the 29th went away better than expected. The kind of consolation or peace of mind that the idea of Providence was giving me served as a sedative. Also, it is possible that such a continued and prolonged meditation in which the strictly personal preoccupations had gone, so to say, to a second plane, overcome by general and metaphysical considerations, might have contributed to tranquilize a little the painful sentiments of my soul. The fact that I had rested a couple of hours with tranquility gave me strength and serenity to prepare the breakfast. I remember very well that I made myself a very strong coffee, since I was determined to proceed forward with calm and method, as rigorously as possible, my general reflections. I was well provided with tobacco, and I must tell you that that day, the 29th, I smoked desperately, almost continuously.

I am piling up perhaps ridiculous details, because the decisive moment is coming and I wish you to have present all details potentially helpful to make your own judgement. I would tell you also that that day I came out for lunch to a little nearby restaurant for workers; that I ate well and with gusto. I came back right away home and had a cup of coffee, also very strong. On the other hand, at the time of dinner, I did not have the energy or wish to get out to the street again. There were at home some canned food. I ate a few crackers with *foie-gras* and had another cup of coffee, also very strong, but with a couple of spoonfuls of condensed milk. I told you already that I did not stop smoking. Physically I was feeling very well; I had no body pain of any kind, and, neither before nor after the event, was there any change in this perfect state of equilibrium in my body.

And, talking now of physical and bodily aspects, let me tell you that I had never suffered any nervous disturbances, except twice in my life: once, in 1910 (I was then twenty four years old), being in Germany; I felt fatigued by the intellectual efforts, and I went to spent the summer to a little island in the North, called Amrun. I had there a nervous attack, losing consciousness, and the local physician diagnosed epilepsy. The diagnosis was wrong because when I returned to Berlin, frightened, and came to the office of doctor Lewandoswsky, he did refute satisfactorily the previous diagnosis and attributed everything, without hesitation, to the state of intellectual fatigue in which I was. There remained within me for a few weeks a small agoraphobia, which soon disappeared. The second time was in 1914, few hours after the birth of my daughter María Pepa. I felt also very tired physically and intellectually, and the nervous stress, due to the long delivery of my wife, was, no doubt, the cause of a very light attack, which, in all likelihood, was also due to fatigue. Since then, I have not had anything at all of the kind.

The Extraordinary Event

At the morning of 29th April, I was placidly serene, meditating or, better, reflecting on that what was preoccupying me so much intellectually. Step by step, I was accepting the providentialist idea and I arrived at the point of formulating it to myself clearly and explicitly. But still my thoughts and my imagination were moving through purely abstract and metaphysical roads. I was thinking of God; but always of the God of deism, the God of pure philosophy, in that intellectual God of which you think but to which you do not pray. A humane and transcendent God, inaccessible, pure, very distant, a mere object of the intellectual investigation. I was considering him in his providence, yes, but his providence as an infinite power with which man has no other relationship than a total, mute, immobile reverence, that *absolute dependence* with which Schleiermacher defines the religious feeling.

In this relatively placid and serene environment, I began to think that the only attitude congruent with that impersonal Providence was that of simple resignation, complete submission, and I disposed myself in my inner self to adopt it. But my efforts were not successful in this respect; a kind of dryness or rigidity which, little by little, became hostility and animosity, a withdrawal of my soul, as if offended by the inaccessible attitude of that metaphysical God, was presenting itself in front of me. In my soul, there took hold a kind of protest, and, I think, God, pardon me, something like a blasphemy rose up to my mind. I think I accused his providence of being indifferent, sarcastic; that Providence which pleased itself in convulsing my life, bringing it up and throwing it down according to inexplicable whims, in bringing and attributing facts and events to it which I did not want, but repudiated. What can I expect –I thought– from a God who pleases himself in playing with me, which sweetens me with the expectation of an imminent perspective of happiness, to take it away from me at the same moment that I was beginning to touch it with my hands? If God is the author of the events of the life of men and He attributes and gives those events to man, I, on my part, can reject that gift. True, that life is not mine, but of a provident God; but it is mine on the other hand, since those events happen to me. Now, I can take them or reject them, and definitively I don't want them; I do not submit myself to the destiny that God wants give to me; I do not want anything to do with God, with that inflexible, cruel and pitiless God.

It was like a fury, a tempest of anger which shook my soul; the fury of an impotent discontent. It seemed to me that there was only one thing I was free to do to make clear my opposition to that Providence which showed itself to be so inaccessible and hostile: to take my own life. That way the Stoics contemplated suicide, as a supreme act of human freedom.

But as soon as I realized the conclusion at which I had arrived, I was frightened. Not because of the idea in itself, which at other occasions had entered my consciousness, but, rather, because of the absolute uselessness of an act which in practice did not solve anything and solved even less the theoretical, metaphysical problem I was attempting to solve. And that astonishment was mainly the terror of having succumbed, or being on the verge of succumbing, to a mental abnormality. Seriously, I began to worry about the possibility of my beginning to talk to myself incoherently.

In fact, I had reached the bottom of an alley with no exit. I told myself that it was necessary to turn back and review again the whole intellectual proceedings that had led me to such a grotesque conclusion. Making a tremendous effort I imposed on myself the task of taking a little rest, a few hours of truce, in my intellectual inquiry. It came then to my mind the idea of putting on the radio to distract me.

They were broadcasting French music: the end of a symphony of César Franck; then, at the piano, the *Pavane pour une infante défunte*, de Ravel; then, an orchestra, playing a piece of Berlioz, entitled *L'enfance de Jésus*. You cannot imagine what this piece is if you don't know it: something exquisite, gentle, of such a delicacy and tenderness, that nobody could listen to it with dry eyes. A magnificent tenor, with very sweet, flexible, smooth, velvet voice, was singing it, modulating incomparably the pure, unaffected, truly divine melody.

When the piece ended, I turned off the radio to avoid disturbing the delicious peace in which the music had subsumed me. Through my mind –without any possibility of any resistance on my part–, began to parade images from my childhood of our Lord Jesus

Christ. I saw Him, in my imagination, walking hand in hand with the Holy Virgin, or sitting on a bench and looking with amazed eyes to St. Joseph and the Blessed Virgin Mary. Representations of other periods in the life of the Lord followed: the moment of forgiving the adulterous woman; Magdalene washing and drying with her long hair the feet of our Savior; Jesus tied to the column; the man of Cyrene helping our Lord to carry forward his Cross, the holy women at the Cross. Little by little, all this was opening in my soul the view of Christ, Christ the man, nailed to the Cross, in a promontory dominating an infinite plain full of men, women, children, over which the arms of Our Crucified Lord were extended. And Christ's arms grew, grew, seeming to embrace all that sorrowful humanity and to embrace all with the immensity of his love; the Cross rose to heaven, covering everything and, after, many, many men, women and children, all of them coming up, nobody was left behind; only I was, nailed to the floor, seeing Christ disappearing on high, surrounded by the enormous crowd of those rising with Him; only myself in that landscape already deserted, kneeling, with my eyes looking up, seeing how the last remnants of that infinite glory were moving away.

No little shyness and shame I have to overcome, don José Maria, to tell you all of this. I am comforted by the conviction that I tell this to somebody who understands and that will be able to keep about it a prudent reserve. But, since there are other things, various and greatest, that I want to tell you, please, let me ask God Our Lord the mercy of his assistance so that my story reproduces faithfully the unadorned truth of what took place that night.

I have no doubt that that kind of vision was the product of a fantasy excited by the sweet and penetrating music of Berlioz. But it had so to say a thundering effect in my soul. «This is God, God alive; this is Providence alive» –I said to myself–. This is God, who understands men, who lives with them, suffers with them, who consoles them, who encourages them and brings them salvation. If God had not descended upon the world, if God had not taken human flesh in the world, man could not have been saved, because between God and men, there would always be an infinite distance which could never be overcome. I had experienced it myself a few hours before. I had attempted with all my sincerity and all my devotion to embrace God, God's Providence; I had wanted to give myself to that Providence who does and undoes the lives of all men. And what had happened? Simply the distance between my poor humanity and that theoretical God of the Philosophy had turned out to be impassable. Too far away, too alien, too abstract, too geometrical and too inhuman. But Christ, God made man, Christ suffering, as I do, more than I do, much more than I do, Himself, I understand, and He understands me. To Him I can filially give my will after this life. To Him I can ask, because I know well He knows what is asking, and I know that He gives and that He will always give; because He has given Himself entirely to us men. Let us pray, let us pray! And then, on my knees, I began to babble the *Our Father*. And, horror!, don José María, I had forgotten it!

I remained on my knees for a long while, offering myself mentally to Our Lord Jesus Christ with the first words which came to me. I remembered my childhood; I remembered my mother, whom I lost when I was nine years old: I represented to myself clearly her face, the lap in which I did recline my head, on my knees, to pray with her; slowly, with patience, I was remembering parts of the *Our Father*; some in French, but after translating them I recovered faithfully the complete Spanish text. After an hour of efforts I succeeded in reconstructing in its integrity the sacred text and I wrote it in a little notebook. I did the same with the *Ave Maria*. But I could not go further. The *Credo* resisted me completely, and the same thing happened with the *Salve* and the *Our Lord Jesus Christ*. I had to remain contented with the *Our Father* —which I was reading in my piece of paper–, insecure of remembering a text so hardly restored, and the *Ave Maria*, which I repeated many, many times, till both prayers remained perfectly engraved in my memory.

An immense peace took over my soul. It is truly extraordinary and incomprehensible how such a profound transformation can be realized in such a short time. Or is it that the transformation has taken place in the subconscious for a much longer time without noticing? In that case the conscious realization would be simply the last step –the only conscious step– of a previous evolution, underground and unconscious.

Be it as it may, the fact was that I saw myself as another man. How exact is Saint Paul's sentence about the two men! But I was still like a horse just broken, trembling, undecided, not knowing what to do, unable to do anything. To go to a church? It was too late and all the churches would surely be closed. To look for a priest? I did not know any in Paris, and also, an invincible shame, an unconquerable shyness, impeded me from talking about these things with anybody except with Christ Himself.

I walked up and down the room, touching my arms, my face, my head. I walked the whole flat not looking for anything, with no object, with no purpose. In my friend Selgas' room, I looked at myself in the mirror, and I stayed, contemplating myself for a long while. I found myself different, in spite of seeing that evidently I was the same. I began to feel something like an unfolding of my personality. Myself in the mirror was the other, the one of yesterday, the one of one thousand years ago; the one inside me, on the other hand, the new one, seemed to me so tender, so fragile, that the least bump could fragment it into one thousand pieces. I came back to my room. Suddenly I thought of my daughters. «When I tell them, what a tremendous emotion!». But, immediately, I resolved not to tell them anything in writing. The only idea of speaking with somebody of all this which had occurred to me, made me shrink irresistibly.

I then sat on a large chair in front of the window, and, through the window, I was seeing all Paris and at the background the dark mass of Montmartre. *Mons Martyrum*! Images of the primitive Christianity came to my mind: the Roman Circus, the lions, the Christians kneeling in the arena, letting themselves be broken into pieces heroically! God's grace inundated, surrounded and supported them. Yes, no doubt; but, besides, they themselves received and accepted that grace and everything God was sending them. Obediently and freely! Because it was very clear they knew what they were doing and what they were willing when they conformed themselves with what God was willing of them.

With all these considerations, it seemed to me that finally I was arriving at last to the best solution to the problem of that life *in* myself and *out* of myself. That life and those facts of life, which provident God does and produces, God gives to us and attributes to us too. But we accept them and receive them *freely*, and because of that they are ours as much as theirs. They are *theirs* because He is Author, creator, distributor and producer. They are *ours* because we accept them from his hand freely. Here is the touch, here is the essence of its Humanity: to accept at the same time submissively and freely. The most proper and the most truly human action is the free acceptance of God's will. The animal accepts God's will because, not being free, it cannot avoid accepting it. Or, to say it better, does not accept, but receives it, the animal finds it upon himself without having thought or without thinking about it. To will freely what God wills! Here is the supreme summit of the human condition. «Thy will be done on earth as it is in heaven».

And kneeling, I lost sight of the far away horizon of the houses of Paris! I recited with intimate devotion once again the *Our Father*, delivering all my will into the wounded hands of Our Lord Jesus Christ.

In the little clock of the wall sounded twelve o'clock. The night was serene and very clear. There reigned in my soul an extraordinary peace. It seemed to me that I was smiling. I sat down again in the big chair and began to think slowly and calmly on my new condition and on the way of life I should adopt. As if I were to ready myself joyfully for a long cherished travel! «The first thing I'll do tomorrow will be to buy a prayer book and a good handbook of Christian doctrine. I'll learn the prayers: I'll instruct myself as well as possible in the dogmatic truths, trying to accept them with the innocence of a child, in other words, without discussing and pondering them for the moment. I will have more than enough time when my faith is solid and robust and it is above any vacillation to rebuild my philosophical castle on new grounds. I'll buy the *Holy Gospels* and a life of Jesus. Jesus! Goodness! Mercy! A white figure, a gesture of love, of pardon, of universal tenderness, Jesus!».

Here there is a hole in my recollections, so minute that I probably fell asleep. My memory recovers the thread of the events at the moment I woke up under the impression of an inexplicable startling event. I cannot say exactly what I felt: fear, anguish, apprehension, presentment of something immense, formidable, ineffable, which was going to take place right away. I stood, trembling, and I opened the window completely. A mouthful of fresh air hit my face.

I turned my face to the interior and became petrified. He was there. I did not see Him, I did not hear Him, I did not touch Him. But He was there. In the room was no other light than that from a minute electric lamp, one with two candles, in one corner. I did not see anything, I did not hear anything, I did not touch anything, I had not the least sensation. But He was there. I remained motionless clenched by the emotion. And I perceived Him; I perceived his presence with the same clarity with which I perceive the paper on which I am writing and the letters –black on white– I am drafting. But I had no sensation either in my sight, my hearing, my touch, my smell or my taste. However I was perceiving Him present there, with absolute clarity. And there was not the least doubt that it was He, since I perceived Him, albeit without sensations. How was this possible? I don't know. But I know that He was there present and that I, without seeing, hearing, smelling or tasting anything, perceived Him with absolute, indubitable evidence. If it were demonstrated to me that it was not Him or that I was delirious, I may have nothing to reply to that demonstration, but, as soon as the remembrance of it is activated again in my memory, it will come back within me the conviction that it was He, because I have perceived Him.

I don't know how long I remained motionless and as hypnotized before his presence. I know that I had no wish of moving and that I would have wished that it would continue for ever, because his presence overwhelmed me with such an intimate joy that nothing was comparable to the supernatural delight I was feeling. It was like the suppression of all that in the body is heavy and gravitates, a subtlety so delicate of all my matter that it could be said that I had not body, as if I had been transformed into soft breeze. It was a caress infinitely sweet, impalpable, incorporeal, which came forth from Him, surrounded me and held me in the air, like a mother holds her son in her arms. But without any sensation of touch.

How did his stay end there? I don't know either. It ended. In an instant, it disappeared. A fraction of a thousandth of a second, He was still there and I was perceiving Him and I was inundated by that said superhuman joy. A thousandth of a second later, He was not there, nobody else was in the room. I was already feeling my weight on the floor and I felt my members and my body standing up by the natural efforts of my muscles.

How long did his presence last? I have said that I don't know. Trying to compute it in retrospect, I made the following calculation. I must have fallen asleep a little after the moment the twelve bell strokes sounding in the little clock beside the wall. Assuming I slept a couple of hours, my waking up just before the event must have occurred at two in the morning. When He disappeared I fell down on the big chair in front of the open window and I remember perfectly that in front of the house, by the railroad –the *Boulevard Sérurier* is at the east end of Paris– there appeared a train *coming up*. A few days later I came quietly to find out and I confirmed that at three and minutes in the morning there came up daily to that station a merchandises train. According to this, his presence must have lasted a little more than an hour. Which is confirmed, more or less, by my recalling much later hearing the four bell strokes in the little clock beside the wall. I suppose, therefore, that his presence began at two and ended at three in the morning. But this calculation may be erroneous. It may be that I did sleep more than two hours, and that his presence began much later than at two. It may be that the train had come delayed. It may be, consequently, that his presence had not lasted more than a few minutes or even a very brief instant. About it, I don't have any firm conviction.

Now let me tell about the infinite reflections I myself objectively and serenely have made on the event, some of them may help you perhaps to make a judgment.

Concluding reflections

The psychological formulation of the *Event* could be the following: *a perception without sensations*. No doubt, in good psychological science, a perception without sensations is very difficult to conceive. Sensations are not lacking even in an hallucination. It follows from the act of perceiving a presence, or the presence of an object, that that act is a human complex act, in which the sensory corporal organs, the senses, intervene necessarily, while an hallucination implies a subjective operation of the psychophysical apparatus, without any actual objective reality present. But the Event I lived is characterized by the total absence of sensations. It would be said a perception by the soul alone, without any help of the body conditioning it. And if I were to withdraw from it the name of perception, call it as you wish; in any case, the event was an intuition of a presence lacking any corporeal condition (sensation).

Since the Event lived by me does not go away from my spirit, and there has been no day from the time I experienced it that I have not remembered it or thought of it, little or much, it is not strange that I am always alert in my readings to see something described resembling somehow what I experienced.

Not long ago I read a passage of Saint Theresa in which she describes something resembling it. It is in chapter XXVII of her *Life*, and says: «Being me in prayer one day to the glorious Saint Peter, I saw by my side, or, better, I felt, because neither with the eyes of the body, nor with the eyes of the soul did I see anything, but it seemed to me that I was at the side of my Christ and it seemed to me that He was talking to me [...]. Later I became very weary to my confessor to tell him. He asked me how did I see him. And I told him that I was not seeing Him. He asked me how did I know then that he was Christ. I told him that I did not know how, but I could not cease believing He was by my side and I saw and felt it clearly...».

You must take into account that the terminology of Saint Theresa lacks psychological rigor; that explains the apparent contradiction in the text when she says that *she did not see Him*, and a few lines after that *she saw Him*. Because when she said she did not see Him, she meant that she had no *visual sensation*, and when she says that she *saw Him clearly and felt Him,* she meant that she perceived Him and had an intuition of Him without sensations.

The event described here by the Saint is then just what I lived, a perception without sensations, or –if you allow me a daring formula– a purely spiritual perception. There are, however, profound differences between what was lived by the Saint and what was lived by me. To the Saint, Our Lord speaks, no doubt, with words received *without* any sound sensation. To me, on the other hand, no. To the Saint, the presence of Our Lord accompanies her for a long time, days and days, in other words, habitually –«It seemed to me Jesus Christ was walking always by my side»–. To me, no. It was only for a short time, perhaps seconds, perhaps minutes, perhaps an hour, in the night from 29th to 30th April 1937. And it has never repeated itself again. On the other hand, my experience has something I have not seen described in that of the Saint. In my experience there is a certain effect produced in me by the presence of the Lord, the effect of de-gravitation, or becoming weightless, of volatilizing; it seemed to me that I became then dispossessed of my body, that I became weightless, that I became a pure blow or that somebody did hold me in the air. About this effect I find nothing in the description of the Saint.

The Saint attempts, also at the end, an *interpretation* of the state she has described, and she finds for it some formulations which I find very fortunate and exact. For instance: «It seemed to me that it was like a person who is in the dark, who does not see another person side by side with her, or, if she is blind, she does not see well. Some likeness it has, but not much, because being blind she can feel with her senses, or hear his speaking or can touch him. Here (on the other hand) *there is nothing of this sort*, there is no darkness to be seen, but *a representation noticed by the soul* more luminous than the sun...». It is perfect the representation of the Saint as *a notice of the soul*, or, as I said before, a purely spiritual perception, *sine corpore interposito*.

The possibility of such events can only be denied by psychologists who are chained to a purely naturalistic, human, interpretation of mystical events.

But one thing is that such an event could be possible and another that I had effectively and really experienced the presence of Our Lord. Please, understand well what I want to say. It is absolutely true that I have experienced what I have described. It is also true, to my mind, absolutely true, that *in itself* what I have described to you is a lived experience of Our Lord being present. Now, is this intrinsic possibility, also extrinsic and real? In other words: although what occurred to me can, *in any person in general*, be the spiritual perception of Our Lord present, can it be so in my case, in particular? Here is the problem.

I do not doubt for an instant that the Lord can, if He wills, present Himself to a soul in that incorporeal fashion, without sensations, without a sensible body interposed. But I have very strong reasons to think that *me, precisely me* Our Lord could not have chosen for such a distinguished mercy, because, what had I done to deserve it? Nothing. I had done too much wrong to deserve it. In other words, that not only was I in a state absolutely deprived of merits to receive such a mercy, but that I was in a *negative* state, in a *positively* bad state.

Nobody better than myself –excepting Our Lord Himself, who knows everything– knows how much a sinner, how much radically perverted I have been in my natural depths. All the anger, all the scale of the most abject sins experienced by my soul. With the aggravation of a doctrinal and ideological superstructure that hid them under the false blanket of a human, natural ethics, more or less philosophical and rational, crowned with an absurd and impious conception of God and its Providence. To such a man was God our Lord to present Himself and to spread over him such extraordinary mercies?

If the Event had been preceded by a long and continuous series of years spent in penance and prayer, in perfect contrition, fed by the Sacraments, it might be perhaps plausible to think that Our Lord were willing to grant the charity of a benevolent look to a loyal serf. But so suddenly, it is quite incredible. How? Why on earth a perverse soul, far from God, who feels an afternoon, almost casually, a little moment of conversion, but nothing else, would deserve to be regaled by God with such mercy? I cannot admit it. I am inclined to think that even if what occurred to me could be taken in itself as a living experience of Our Lord present, it was no such a thing in my particular and concrete case. Therefore what happened to me was a pure fantasy, a pure imagination, due to an abnormal pathological state of my subjectivity, or was a diabolic fiction.

But, thinking serenely, on the other hand I find grave difficulties with this last conclusion. Because a diabolic fiction it does not seem at all to me to be. As a matter of fact, it is not conceivable in an event that produces such consequences as the Event produced in my soul: an unbreakable resolution, kept till today without any dismay –may God go on feeding it with his grace!–, and, through one thousand difficulties and obstacles, a firm decision of devote myself to God's service all my life state as his minister; a grace that was conserved till becoming sanctifying grace when on 29th June 1938, I received what I now call my second First Communion, from my Bishop, in Vigo; a perseverance which has been victorious until now –may God keep protecting me!– of all inconveniences. Is it possible that a cause which produces such effects be diabolic?

But, if we keep to one side the diabolic hypothesis, it remains only that I have been deceived very much by my own subjectivity, and that the Event lived by me is but the subjective effect of a deep mental crisis. No doubt, in all that preceded, accompanied and followed the Event, I cannot trace the least hint of abnormality, nor have I ever felt in myself pathological elements of a psychic character, except the two nervous breakdowns that I mentioned to you before. Precisely those two attacks were characterized by their exclusively somatic character, with no trace of psychic disorder, and were only physiological, nervous, without any influence on the mental, representative or imaginative capacity. I had never had hallucinations, nor mental complexes, nor excessive hyper excitations, nor, in sum, any perturbation in my psychic life. No psychiatrist examining me could find a basis to diagnose the least psychic sickness. None of the persons who know me or have known me from my childhood could ever believe that I am a mentally perturbed person.

I have however an imagination and a sensibility perhaps stronger than what is common, a circumstance which causes me to have moral pains and interior reactions stronger than it is convenient. And even if I generally master and control that sensibility and imagination, which a self-critical faculty of self-observation, philosophical study and solitary meditations have developed in me, it is not unlikely on the contrary, but very likely, that on very exceptional occasions, like this unique occasion of profound crisis previously described, touching and badly repressed, formless concretions may have precipitated in me, leading me to a kind of hallucination without concomitant sensations. I find no other way of explaining what I experienced on that unforgettable night. I resist resolutely to think that God had deigned Himself to grant but a minute of his presence to me, so depraved and so miserable.

At most I could assume perhaps that God willed to secure my conversion with such a profound grace engraved so unforgettably in my soul, allowing it to take place in my mind that subjective phenomenon whose indelible memory would help me to persevere victoriously against all the ambushes, difficulties and inconveniences that necessarily would oppose my vocation.

This is the main object of my consultation to you, don José María. To nobody in the world, even during confession, have I ever spoken of the things contained in this long relation. I have no thought, or wish of ever talking with anybody about it, unless you order it to me. More: I feel such a deep timidity and shame at these things, that in the one year since I put myself under your direction, I have not dared until now to tell even you anything about it. My deepest wish would be to know your opinion and counsel, and then never to come back to talk about it even with you.

Before finishing, it is convenient perhaps that you know some later circumstances related to the Event.

Already more than three years are gone by since it occurred. Since then I have not noticed anything which could be extraordinary or supernatural states. My life has gone on its normal and robust course. I have offered to God all moral sufferings which, of course, my conversion has brought to me, which have not been negligible. Always, the memory of the Event has meant for me an extraordinary and reflective consolation and has served to me as a shield, helping me to come out victorious from all difficulties and adversities.

At the beginning, in other words, it has gone approximately one year and half after it occurred, I wished occasionally that something more or less similar would be repeated in me, and at times, but few, I asked it from God. But already before knowing you, I had cancelled definitely those wishes and petitions. Submitted to God's will I do not wish or ask anything like this; more: I fear the idea that something like that may repeat itself, and what I ask God is that that peace of soul I have achieved be not perturbed. My only aspiration and my constant petition is that Our Lord keeps my faith, in which, since then, I have not faltered for a moment, even when I began the study —so dangerous for me— of dogmatic theology. That He conserves my faith in its integrity and that He gives me his grace to serve Him with honesty and fidelity, with total dedication to the limit of my already scarce forces. That He conserves in my soul the peace I enjoy now and that, to my mind, it will not be easy to be perturbed, if God's protection does not abandon me.

Let me add a few concrete data for you. The following day after the Event I made the resolution of consecrating myself to God and to embrace the priestly state. But, since the future was so obscure and dark and uncertain, and there was no room, in those days of May 1937, of making definitive commitments, taking also into account that I needed to evaluate and purify my soul and test its capacity of perseverance, I prudently delayed all exterior manifestation.

On 3rd May I received a letter from my daughters, who were already in Barcelona, in the house of our good relatives. Then, seeing that the war was for long, I thought that it would be best to abandon Paris and reduce myself to as much solitude and retreat as was then possible. My work on the dictionary, with which I earned my sustenance, could be made in any other suitable place. I remembered that a friend of mine, l'abbé Pierre Jobit, who was living then in Angouleme –he resides at present in Madrid– was very familiar with the Benedictines of Ligugé Abbey, near Poitiers. That place, which I knew since a visit as a tourist, I liked very much because it was retired, leafy and peaceful. I wrote to l'abbé Jobit and, through him, I got into written communication with the abbot of Ligugé, who was so kind as to be willing to receive me in his convent. I was getting ready to make the trip when I received the news of the immediate arrival of my daughters in Paris.

In the interim, in the first fortnight of May, Largo Caballero's government fell, being substituted by the government of Dr. Negrín. In this new government, there did not figure Galarza, the main author of the negative to the exit of my daughters. My friends in Paris recommended to me that, since Negrín had previously shown himself favorable to my wishes, I should renew my petition, now, that, being President of the Council, it would be easier for him to act, if he, in effect, was willing to please me. Without much confidence I wrote directly to Negrín a letter, which remained without response. I was giving up the matter for lost and, having no reason to hope, I had almost completed my preparations for moving to the monastery of Ligugé, when I received a telegram from Barcelona announcing that my daughters were already leaving for France, and saying that they would telegraph me from Cerbère.

As a matter of fact, the following day I received a telegram from Cerbère with the hour of their arrival in Paris.

On 9th June I had the immense joy of embracing my daughters and grandchildren. I found myself heading a family of six adult persons and two children. There was no other solution but to go to America. I delayed everything else. In a few days, the trip to Buenos Aires was fixed, I received the money and obtained the passports. On 20th June, we embarked from Marseilles. On 10th July, we arrived in Buenos Aires. On 17th we arrived in Tucuman. I began immediately my conferences and classes. I began them but, inside, I was literally terrified. The test imposed on my incipient faith and my problematic perseverance was extremely hard. I was earning much. They were paying me well. We were living comfortably, more than comfortably: we were saving money. On the other hand, I had to teach two subjects: one was general Philosophy, and the other Psychology. What dangers! What ambushes! How easy to slide again towards the old roads that, so dramatically, I had just abandoned!

I don't want to abuse more your patience, don José María. It suffices to tell you, that, with God's help, I triumphed over all those dangers. I tried –I think successfully– to give to my courses in the University of Tucuman an anodyne character regarding problems touching matters coincident with our Holy Religion. I kept my secret so carefully that even my daughters did not notice.

Eleven months after arriving in Tucuman, in other words, in May 1938, I said farewell to the University. With what I had saved and a *tournée* of lectures, very lucrative, I did throughout Montevideo, Buenos Aires, Rosario, Panamá, Cordoba and Santa Fe, I got sufficient money to take care of my trip to Spain and to keep a remnant capable of sustaining my family and me for a full year. I did not expect the war to last longer.

I wrote a very long letter to Monsignor the Bishop –with whom, since 1930 I had had very good personal relations –uncovering to him my plans, telling him all the details of my conversion, but not alluding at all to the extraordinary Event which I have just referred to you. The Bishop answered by cable, approving everything and giving me his heartfelt congratulation. We embarked from Buenos Aires on 3rd June. We arrived to Lisbon on the night of the 27th. Already during the trip I had informed my daughters of my new being as a Christian and even of my will to be a future priest. They cried with me of joy.

On the 28th in the morning I embraced my Bishop with great emotion. On the same 28th in the afternoon I made a confession with him, a general confession. In it, while it was very long and detailed, I could not dare to tell him about the extraordinary Event which has been the object of this account. It did not seem to me necessary, and an invincible timidity restrained me without remedy. On the 29th in the morning, in the chapel of Atalaya de Castro, where the Bishop lived, we all attended Mass, said by him, and I received the Holy Communion from his hands, with my cheeks wet by thick tears. Two months and a half later, 10th September 1938, I entered the convent of the Mercedary Fathers of Poyo, and began thereby formally my preparation for the priesthood.

September, 1940. *Laus Deo.*

AZAÑA

Manuel Azaña (1880-1940), born into a wealthy family in Alcalá de Henares, became an orphan at a very young age. He went to secondary school in Madrid at *Instituto Cisneros*. He studied also at the Augustinians, El Escorial, and at the Central University, Madrid. He obtained the Licentiate degree of Law (a degree intermediate between the Bachelor's and the Master's degrees) by the University of Saragossa, and a Doctorate by the University of Madrid (Complutense) in 1900.

Azaña became a critic of General Primo de Rivera's dictatorship and, in 1924, he signed a strong manifesto attacking King Alphonse XIII and the dictator.

In 1930, he was one of the signatories of the *Pact of San Sebastián*, put together by all republicans and separatists against Primo de Rivera.

In the municipal elections of April 1931, republican candidates had the majority in Madrid, Barcelona and a few other large Spanish cities. The monarchist candidates won in the whole country. In spite of that, the republicans proclaimed their victory. Alcalá Zamora, self appointed Prime Minister of the provisional government of the Second Republic (the short lived First Republic had had four presidents in less than a year before collapsing) named Azaña Minister of War on 14th April 1931. When the new Constitution was approved on 9th December, Alcalá Zamora became President, and Azaña substituted him as Prime Minister, as the leader of the coalition of Left-wing parties which included Azaña's own *Acción Republicana* and the Socialists (PSOE).

Azaña's government did little to reform the taxation system to shift the burden to the wealthy. He confronted mercilessly the anarchist CNT (Confederación Nacional de los Trabajadores) when violence erupted in Casas Viejas, Castilblanco and Arnedo. Azaña's extreme and arbitrary anti-Catholic policies caused very soon the alienation of a large sector of the Spanish population. He was focused, from the first moment, in antagonizing and dismantling the Spanish Army, which had a long tradition of patriotism and loyalty to spiritual values.

In the General Elections of November held in 1933 the Left was heavily defeated. Azaña's party got 5 deputies instead of 26 and the Radical Socialists 4 instead of 56. However, even after the clear electoral defeat, Azaña and the republican Left refused to leave power. In those 1933 Elections the conservative Right and center Right had obtained an unquestionable victory: five millions votes against three to their opponents. This majority which was even more clearly reflected in the seats at the Parliament.

Azaña's conflicts with Right and extreme Left forced him to call for a vote of confidence in the Parliament. Two thirds of the Cortes abstained. Then Alcalá Zamora ordered finally Azaña's resignation on 8th September 1933. After the elections, Azaña and the Left threatened violence if the conservative CEDA (Confederacón Española de Derechas Autónomas) –the clear winners– dared to form government. He was willing to tolerate only a joint government CEDA-Radical Socialists presided by Alejandro Lerroux. In 1934, Azaña founded a new party, the Left Republican Party, with the Republican Socialists of Marcelino Domingo, and the Galician ORGA (Organización Republicana Gallega Autónoma) of Santiago Casares Quiroga.

On 5th October 1934, the PSOE, the Communists and the Basque and Catalonian Separatists called for a general Left-wing rebellion which became in fact the clarion call for the Spanish Civil War. The 1934 rebellion succeeded, temporarily, only in Asturias, where the Socialist winners gained control and kept it for two weeks. They committed all kind of atrocities. Thirty priests and many civilians were killed in such that short time. Azaña apparently was not directly implicated, but he was arrested and charged with complicity. He was imprisoned and then released in 1935. Immediately he organized the *Popular Front* (Frente Popular), a coalition of all major Left-wing parties, including Socialists, Communists and even Anarchists, which in previous elections had recommended abstention.

On 16th February 1936 the united Left won a quarrelsome General Elections by a very narrow margin. But, once the new Cortes convened, the Left managed to transform a narrow majority in an overwhelming one. Everything was ready now for a Soviet style revolution, headed by Largo Caballero, the radical leader of the Socialist Party (PSOE), who was proud of being called the *Spanish Lenin*.

Pío Moa, in *Los Mitos de la Guerra Civil* (La Esfera de los Libros: Madrid, 2003), summarizes well Azaña's role in the events which led to the war. He had said: «Everybody fits in the Republic... [but the Republic] should be thought of and governed only by the republicans». Obviously, when later Azaña was accusing the conservatives of being undemocratic, he forgot that he had been still more undemocratic. He further said: «I laugh when the specter of the social clash is raised [...]. I would not (in such a case) call for moderation from this tribune [the Cortes]». With all his dialectical skills, which were considerable, he pushed the prohibition in Spain of all religious orders devoted to teaching, in a country where the Catholic religion was loved or at least respected by a large fraction of the citizenry. And he added: «Don't tell me that this is against personal freedom... This is a matter of public health», adding: «All churches in Madrid are not worth the life of a republican».

All along the 19th century the Spanish Left used various labels: *exalted, liberals, progressives*, and finally *republicans*. The leaders of the anti-Catholic Left were relatively few, but they managed *to carry the cat to the water* at critical times.

For Azaña the lay republic (*república laica*) consisted in the leftist *intelligentsia* backed by what he called the *gross popular battalions* (socialists, anarchists...). But he had to learn that these *popular battalions* were utterly refractory to follow the leadership of the *intelligentsia*.

In his diaries Azaña laments the incredible stupidity of most republican leaders and treats them with contempt: Gordón Ordás, the radical socialist chief, was a *pedantic failure*; Marcelino Domingo was a *good for nothing*; Álvaro de Albornoz, a *simpleton who knows nothing*, etc, etc.

Ángel Palomino, in *Caudillo* (Planeta: Barcelona, 1992), attributes the following words to Azaña: «Franco did not rebel against the Republic; he rebelled against the *chusma* (rabble), which had usurped power in the Republic». I have tried to locate the source of this quotation with Pío Moa, very familiar with Azaña's prolific writings, but unsuccessfully. But he told me that these words reflect very well Azaña's thought at the end.

Azaña died in exile in Montauban (France) on 4th November 1940, when Germany had half France occupied and the Vichy Government ruled in Montauban. The French authorities did not allow his coffin being covered by the Spanish Republican flag at his burial and. It was finally covered with the flag of Mexico, the country which had hosted many Spanish Republicans in their exile.

JOSÉ DÍAZ AND *EL CAMPESINO*

According to Pío Moa, the two *icons* of the Spanish Communist Party during the Spanish Civil War were José Díaz, General Secretary from 1932 to 1939, and Dolores Ibárruri, *La Pasionaria*, the eloquent speaker and fiery agitator who galvanized the masses during the War years. Another *icon*, not always obedient to the Party's rule for very long was Valentín González, *El Campesino*, whose bravery and natural gifts as a commander brought him up quickly to the rank of lieutenant commander in the Spanish Red Army early in the war.

In contrast with the PSOE and the CNT, the PCE (Spanish Communist Party) acted consistently as a monolithic and disciplined block under the iron-clad higher direction of Moscow.

As Dimitroff declared in the 7th Congress of the Soviet Komintern, the Spanish Popular Front should be seen as the waiting room for the Socialist revolution. In the 7th Congress José Díaz was a member of the executive committee, and Largo Caballero was hailed as the leader who would carry on the Soviet Revolution into the Iberian Peninsula. He had been criticized by the communists not so long ago, but in 1936 he earned for himself the support of the PCE against Indalecio Prieto. It should be recalled that the thirties were the years of the bloody Soviet *purges* in Russia, a time when the land workers were mercilessly decimated in Russia by Stalin and his collaborators.

At that time José Díaz was saying on record:

> [Russia] has become the first country in the world as culture is concerned –the workers' culture in the Soviet Union is well above the rest–; [Russia] has become the second industrial country of the world –the first in Europe– and will be the first in the world in a short time; [Russia] has provided wealth fare for the land workers and today has an army, the Glorious Red Army, which has deserved because of its own merits the respect of the entire world. There [in Russia], scientists, men of learning, intellectuals have no barriers to develop their research, [etc, etc, etc].

At that time the PCE was achieving its major triumphs in Spain. The CGTU (the Communist syndicate, very small before in comparison with the UGT and the CNT) joined the Socialist UGT, and also the PCE managed to merge its youth organization with the youth of the PSOE, to its advantage. It was the time when the very young Santiago Carrillo began to escalate positions in the Spanish political scenery.

José Díaz, as Secretary General of the PCE, in March 1937, tried to play down the hostility between Communists and Anarchists in Barcelona, where the Anarchists were specially strong. He said: «Our enemies are circulating the lie that a bloody clash between Communists and Anarchists is unavoidable [...]. Those who are propagating these lies are our enemies as well as the enemies of our Anarchist comrades». But he did so to no avail. George Orwell, in his *Homage to*

Catalonia, vividly demonstrates that these were not lies. The bloody clash between Communists and Anarchists took place in Barcelona. It was one of the main reasons of the final defeat of the reds.

After the Civil War, José Díaz moved to the Soviet Union. In the morning of 19th March 1942, in Tiflis, he fell down from his room in a fourth floor, and died instantly. Silence surrounded the circumstances of his death for some time, but rumors that he had committed suicide began soon to circulate. Questioned about it, those Spaniards who were with him at Tiflis answered: «They have killed him». His origins had been in Andalusian anarcho-syndicalism. Moscow's propaganda had made of him an international leader, but after the war he had ceased to be useful to Stalin.

Valentín González, *El Campesino*, was born in Malcocinado (Extremadura) in 1904. He was the son of an Anarchist day laborer and he worked as a miner since very young. Later he became a fugitive of the Civil Guard, before joining the Spanish Legion, from which he deserted. Finally, he joined the PCE. At the beginning of the Civil War he entered the 5th Regiment. His bravery and natural gift for leadership propitiated a quick promotion. At the end of the Civil War, after the defeat of the Republican Army, he escaped to Oran and from there to France and finally to the USSR. There, he entered with the rank of General the Soviet Higher School of War, from which he was soon expelled due to disagreements with Stalin's policies. He was tortured in several *chekas*, including the famous Lubianka, and was condemned to forced labor in the *gulag*. Finally he succeeded in escaping Russia in 1949. He lived then in France till he returned to Spain in 1977.

Valentín González died in Madrid in 1985 where he was a supporter the socialist Felipe González in the first General Elections of 1977.

El Campesino, in his book *Yo Escogí la Esclavitud* (New Edition: Ciudadela Libros: Madrid, 2006), reproduces an interview with Indro Montanelli in Paris, 1950. In the words of Indro Montanelli:

> *El Campesino* was a former hero of Red Spain, a former General of division, a former deported prisoner, and now a former

Communist. Just after his arrival, he declared: «To die would have been for me most pleasant. I wanted to live, on the other hand, to tell the world about the Soviet inferno». They offered him (says Montanelli) refuge in the United States and some believed he had accepted because nothing was known about him for one year. But he had been in Paris with a Persian passport with the name of Caprilla […]. [Forty years old] with his black hair and white teeth, with his penetrating and black eyes, *El Campesino* deserved well his alias […]. A gunman at fifteen years, a deserter at twenty-four, a commander at thirty, condemned and deported for Trotskyist at thirty-five, he had been running very fast in a long distance career, perfectly logical given the premises from which he acted […]. Anarchists the world over should learn from this man and should reflect carefully before believing Moscow's propaganda […]. [Montanelli quotes the words of *El Campesino*]: «When in Moscow they had me at the Lubianka, one day, fellow prisoners asked me how were the prisons in Spain. I told them. They listened to me with wide open eyes, and one of them exclaimed: "But then, what kind of justice were you fighting for in your country if you had it already?". In the interrogatory [at the Lubianka], they wanted me to confess that I was sold to the American capitalists and that (already in Spain), that I was leading my men into combat to get them killed, weakening this way the anti-Franco army». [In fact] *Pasionaria* and Modesto testified [against *him*] corroborating it …

At the end of the interview, when all present raised their glasses of sherry to celebrate, Montanelli pointed out to *El Campesino* the provenance of that sherry, saying: « It is[from] Franco in person». Valentín González, after a moment of vacillation, tasted the liquor and added: «Genuine!».

In his booklet *I Chose Slavery*, Valentín González, *El Campesino,* makes the most eloquent and hard hitting indictment of Soviet Russia under Stalin:

> The Russian people, in my opinion, as much because of nature as because of tradition, is one of the most welcoming and fraternal peoples on Earth. If it sometimes seems brutal and cruel, it is due solely to the misery, ignorance and oppression to which it has been submitted for centuries.
> Under the pretext of a Socialist competition, they have terribly aggravated to crazy extremes the division, the contempt, the cowardice and the rivalry between human beings. The people as

such has disintegrated; in Russia there is no longer anything else but the State and the regime.

Everybody is a tyrant with everybody. The result is that only the strong, the astute and the cynical succeed in surviving. That means that they can save their miserable existence at the expense of their dignity and their conscience...

In all countries there are injustices, but only in the USSR injustice is total, permanent.

Valentín González knows. He was imprisoned in Vorkuta, one of the worst Soviet concentration camps beyond the Polar Circle. *El Campesino*, unlike Líster, Pasionaria, Modesto and Tagüeña, was not subservient to the Soviet system.

He, miraculously, escaped death at Lubianka and at Vorkuta.

PRIETO AND LARGO CABALLERO

Indalecio Prieto (1883-1962) and Francisco Largo Caballero (1869-1946) were the two most conspicuous leaders of the Spanish Socialist Party (PSOE) before, during and immediately after the Spanish Civil War. Prieto liked to see himself as moderate and a liberal, and Largo Caballero, at least since 1934, was pleased to be called the Spanish Lenin. A Lenin, it should be remembered, that had said things like: «Against the bodies, violence; against the souls, deception » – «Words are bullets» – «Take always advantage of fellow travelers and useful idiots». Both Prieto and Largo Caballero were protagonists in the tragedy of the Spanish Civil War. Fortunately, in spite of the massive support of the Soviet Union (well paid by the gold of the Bank of the Spain, of all Spaniards), they were defeated. For the moment, the statues of Prieto and Largo Caballero prominently erected by Felipe González's Government in the 1980's at Madrid's *Nuevos Ministerios* are in place, while Franco's statue, for more than half a century presiding the West entrance of those *Nuevos Ministerios*, is not so since 2005, suppressed by Zapatero's Government.

Let us quote Prieto:

- I am a socialist because I am a liberal (Bilbao, March 1921).

123

- And I tell the enemy: you are already defeated. Be aware of your responsibilities, consider your mistakes. Look inside, look well and see if you find within yourself something impelling you to continue fighting, because don't expect surrender... (On the radio, 24th July 1936).
- The idea that in a war the winning side is the one which has at its disposal more means to resist is very old. A war is not simply heroism, a war is not simply bravery; a war cannot be won by the simple superiority of the human factor; a war is infinitely more; a war is, above all, the means to resist [...]. Think, with me, that the confrontation in which we are actors in the bloody soil of our country is not a simple mutiny, a simple revolt: it is a war. With all the terrible connotations that this word carries with it. Even more than a war: it is a civil war; a war among countrymen, a war a among brothers. And as a war must it be treated.

  On whose side are the greater possibilities of victory in a war? On the side which has more means, which has more [favorable] elements. Well, widely spread, as it is, the military uprising, the means they have at their disposal are inferior to the means of the Spanish State, to the means of the Government.

  There is no other money for the Spanish contenders, once public credit is lost in foreign countries, than gold. All the gold in Spain, all Spanish monetary resources valid outside, all, absolutely all, are in the hands of the Government; they are the gold reserves which have been the guarantee of our paper money. The only one which can dispose of them, because they are in its hands, is the Government...

  But, in addition, today a war is mainly an industrial war. That contender (will win), which has more means to win, which has at its disposal the principal industrial elements... Take a look throughout the map of Spain [...] (On the radio, 8th August 1936).

Let us quote Largo Caballero:

- We don't believe in democracy as in an absolute value. We don't believe in freedom either (Geneva, Summer of 1934).
- I want to tell the Right that if we win we will collaborate with our allies; but if the Right wins, our work will be duplicated, collaborating with our allies within the law, but also committing ourselves to the Civil War. We don't say

something for sake of saying it, we say it because we mean it (Bilbao, 20th January 1936, one month before the February elections).

- The working class must conquer the political power, convinced that democracy is incompatible with socialism, and that since the one who has the power will not surrender it voluntarily, it will be necessary to go to the Revolution (Linares, 20th January 1936).
- The total transformation of the country cannot be achieved introducing ballots into urns [...] we are disgusted with the essays of this democracy; we want our democracy to be installed in the country (Madrid, 10th February 1936).

Largo Caballero recalls in *Mis Recuerdos* (Paris, 1946) the takeover of the Spanish Government by the Communists in 1937:

Prieto, as well as the President, Azaña, were informed in detail about what they [the Communists] were planning. But he [Prieto] lacked the energies to solve the difficult problems with the resolution and the speed required by the circumstances, and he convoked the representatives of the political parties to examine the situation. They leaned to the side of Negrín and the Communists. The one most resolved against Prieto was Gonzalez Peña, President of the Union Party and Secretary of Justice thanks to his protector, Indalecio Prieto, now betrayed by him. How applicable are some Castilian refrains ...: «Raise crows and they will draw out your eyes!». «He who kills by the sword will die by the sword».

News arrived in Barcelona that the rebels were near the Mediterranean Sea, and therefore that Catalonia would be cut from the rest of Spain. As my daughters had been left in Valencia I decided to go by car to pick them up, under grave danger of being captured by the Falangists. Could I leave them in Valencia and remain in Barcelona? Prieto knew about it, and ordered that a plane be put at my disposal for the flight to and back from Valencia. I left the same day and the following day I was back in Barcelona with my daughters.

It would not be honest to silence this good deed of Prieto, and very likely that was the last order he gave as Prime Minister. This favor which I always will remember gratefully may absolve him of all bad deeds done against me, and I would never regret such forgiveness. But he could never be absolved of all the damage inflicted to the Socialist Party, to the Unión General de Trabajadores, and to Spain (Francisco Largo Caballero, *Mis Recuerdos* [Ediciones Alianza: Mexico D.F, Mexico, 1954], pp. 240-41).

MOLA

Emilio Mora Vidal was born in Placetas, Villa Clara (Cuba) on
9th July 1887, and died at an airplane crash in Alcocero (Burgos),
during the Civil War, on 3rd June 1937. He was the head
(*director*) of the civil-military rising which triggered the three
years Civil War ending with the victory of the Nationals (or
Nationalists, as they are called in the English literature on the
Civil War), which resulted in the longest most peaceful and most

constructive period in the last three hundred years of Spanish history.

Mola was military governor at Pamplona in 1936. He was no monarchist but seeing the disaster brought to his country by the 2nd Republic, in spite of having rebelled against the Popular Front Government under the three-colored republican flag, he was moved by the bravery of the Navarrese Carlist volunteers to sympathize with the traditional Catholic monarchy. From July 1936 to June 1937, Mola was the head of the military operations in the North, including the Basque provinces, Alava, San Sebastian and Biscay.

Born in Cuba in 1887, Mola was marked from his youth by the disaster of the Spanish-American War of 1898, which resulted in the lost of Cuba, Puerto Rico and the Philippines for Spain. Mola entered the Military Academy of Toledo in 1904 and was soon sent to the Bailén Regiment of Infantry where he took part in the African War and where he was awarded the Individual Military Medal, one of the higher military distinctions of the Spanish Army, for courage in combat.

In May 1912 he was seriously wounded and was promoted to Captain for war merits. Promoted to Colonel in 1921 for merits of war, he took part in the landing of Alhucemas, in which joint Spanish and French forces ended the War in Africa. In 1927, at forty years, he was promoted to Brigade General and was appointed as military commander of Larache.

After the fall of Primo de Rivera dictatorship, Mola was appointed General Director of Security by the provisional Government and his firm handling of social unrest by socialists and anarchists made him unpopular with the Left. He wrote a letter to his comrade in arms Fermín Galán, who attempted in November 1930 an aborted *coup d'état* to proclaim the 2nd Republic. The Republican uprising ended in disaster.

Police activity under Mola against the frustrated Republican coup made him highly unpopular with Azaña's Republican Government, after 14th April 1031, when finally the Spanish Republic was proclaimed, following King Alphonse XIII's voluntary exile. Azaña ceased Mola and ordered his discharge, suspending him of employment and salary.

In 1934, after the October revolution in Asturias, Franco was able to get Mola's amnesty and reincorporation to active service. In 1935, Mola was appointed Commander of Western Morocco, with see in Melilla. At the end of this year he was promoted to Head of the Military Forces in all Spanish Morocco, based in Tetouan. After the electoral victory of the Popular Front in 1936, several transfers of generals were decreed by the new Government. Mola was named military governor of Pamplona, in command of the 12th Brigade of Infantry, trying to keep him as far away as possible; like Franco, who was named military governor of the Canary Islands. The government made a big mistake with Mola because his presence in Pamplona was critical to mobilize the Navarrese Traditionalists, an essential ingredient in the *Alzamiento* (Rising), as it was essential the mobilization of Falangists in Burgos and Valladolid.

Mola had tense conversations with Manuel Fal Conde, the Carlist leader, who insisted in bringing his men to action only on condition of doing so for the Catholic Traditionalist monarchy, and under the gold and red traditional flag. The count of Rodezno intervened in the last moment, ignoring the Fal Conde's demands. Mola (*El Director*) sent secret instructions to those military units in Spain determined to rise against the Republic. After several delays and detours the date of 18th July 1936 was chosen. The army of Africa, under Franco, rose that day. Mola waited until the 19th. The military rising did not succeed as, in good measure, was anticipated by its leaders in Madrid and Barcelona. Mola and his *requetés*, and with the VII Organic Division, was supposed to control the Northern provinces, including Santander, Burgos, Palencia, Logroño, the Basque provinces, Alava, Biscay, Guipuzcoa and Navarre. But the coup failed in half of these provinces. With his *requetés*, he was able to control Logroño, Alava and Guipuzcoa, taking Irun, at the border with France. After the death of General Sanjurjo, the 20th of July, in an airplane accident at Estoril (Portugal), the rebels controlled three zones. Mola in the North: Galicia, Old Castile, Caceres, Oviedo, Alava, Navarre and the best part of Aragon; Queipo de Llano in the South: Seville, Cordova, Cadiz and parts of other Andalusian provinces; and Franco in Africa, ready to cross the Strait of Gibraltar if the circumstances permitted. Finally the Legionaries and *Regulars* (Moorish troops, excellent combatants) were brought to the peninsula by air (the first aerial bridge in the history of war) and by sea. Franco's men led by Yagüe and Varela progressed to the North very fast at the beginning. After the liberation of the Alcazar of Toledo, the 1st of October, the *Junta de Defensa Nacional* convened in Salamanca and elected Franco *Jefe del Estado,* and the Army's Generalissimo.

Mola, on a broadcasting during the Autumn of 1936, explained how four columns were advancing on the capital; two from the North; two from the South, and, he said, a clandestine *fifth column*, made up of sympathizers of the rebels, was inside, ready to join with the others and conquer Madrid.

When in the Spring of 1937 Mola commanded the attack of the Nationalists on Bilbao, he faced strong resistance from the Basque fighters. Von Sperrle, the General of the German Condor Legion, decreed a massive bombing of Guernica, the symbolic Basque little village. The bombing was not approved by Mola. But the number of victims given by the Republican propaganda was 1,600, while the serious investigation of Salas Larrazábal, quoted in Pío Moa's *The Myths of Spanish Civil War*, reduces it to 120 at most. However, Picasso's painting *Guernica* is the symbol of 20th century cruelty, while Dresden and Hiroshima are not. After the bombing, the German Condor Legion was prohibited any initiative in bombing civil population. It may be noted that Guernica had arms factories in the outskirts.

Red propaganda tried to blame on Franco Mola's death in accident without any objective foundation. It should be noted that in Salamanca, when the decision to appoint Franco Jefe del Estado and Caudillo, Mola was the first to support Kindelán's proposal. A proposal which was immediately accepted unanimous, except by General Cabanellas.

VARELA AND YAGÜE

At the time of the Spanish Civil War, with the world attention focused on the Iberian Peninsula, the names of several Spanish Generals were household names all over, as were the names of Popular Front leaders; Anarchist, Socialist or Communist, like Durruti, *El Campesino* and Líster.

In the Nationalist side two military leaders were outstanding: the Andalusian José Enrique Varela (Carlist, twice decorated in Africa with the *Laureada de San Fernando*) and the Castilian Juan Yagüe (Falangist, who was protagonist of the rapid advance from Cadiz to Madrid, 500 km in only four weeks which almost decided the Civil War at its beginning).

* * *

Varela was born in San Fernando, Cadiz, in 1891, and died in Tangier, Morocco, in 1951. His father, Juan Varela, was a Sergeant and a head of the musical band of the 1st Regiment of Marines in the Spanish Army. When he was 18 years old, he entered the Regiment of his father, and got his dispatch of

Alférez (Second Lieutenant) from the hands of king Alphonse XIII.

Just out of the Military Academy he was sent to Melilla. At the war in Africa he fought bravely at Muires and Ruman in 1920, and then at Adama in 1921, deserving two *Lauredas de San Fernando,* the highest Spanish military decoration. Getting one such decoration is rare. Getting two is really exceptional. He was promoted to Lieutenant Colonel (1926) for war merits, and to Colonel (1929) after receiving *Medalla Militar Individual* (second highest military distinction).

After the proclamation of the Second Spanish Republic, on 14th April 1931, his Carlist (Traditionalist) convictions were reinforced. (He would be later the author of the military Ordinances of the *requetés*). He seconded the Monarchist uprising of General Sanjurjo against the Republic in 1932 and he was made prisoner in Seville after the frustrated coup.

In 1935, after Asturias Revolution, being Gil-Robles Minister of Defense and Franco his Chief of Staff, Varela was promoted to General of Brigade. In the months before February 1936's General Elections, Varela joined other military leaders in their plans to overthrow the Republic. In July 1936 he was among the military leaders cooperating closely with Mola.

At the beginning of the Civil War, on 18th July 1936, Varela, with reinforcements from Morocco, took the city of Cadiz for the Nationalists in the middle of a general strike decreed by the workers leftist syndicates. This was essential to transfer from Africa the Legionaries and *Regulars*. Varela took part, with Queipo de Llano, in the submission of Seville, Antequera, Cordova and other cities in Andalusia. On 24th September he substituted in command to Yagüe in the detour of the advancing forces to liberate the Alcazar of Toledo. Yagüe wanted to push forward to Madrid as soon was possible, but Franco, more cautious, decided to go for Toledo first, well aware of the international resonance of its liberation. After the Nationalist advance on Madrid was stopped, with the help of the International Brigades at the *Ciudad Universitaria*, it was clear that the Civil War was going to be a long one.

Varelatook part in numerous subsequent battles: Jarama, Brunete, Teruel, Aragon and Levant.

He was appointed Minister of the Army in the first of Franco's governments after the war. In 1939-42, he created the Polytechnic School of the Army, the Regiment for the Guard of the Jefe del Estado, the Historic Military Museum, the University Militia, which (like in other countries at that time) provided instruction to University students willing to become junior military officers instead of doing the regular compulsory military service.

On 16th August 1942 at the Basilica of Begoña in Bilbao, Varela suffered an attempt to his life at the hands of José Domínguez, a radical young Falangist likely brainwashed by the Nazis. Varela resulted unharmed, but there were a hundred of wounded. Varela presented his resignation to Franco, but Franco acted immediately and a quick trial resulted in the summary execution of the young Falangist. After the surrender of Italy, Varela, with Kindelán, Orgaz, Solchaga and other generals formally requested Franco's resignation in order to bring back the Monarchy. Franco managed to overcome the difficult situation and remained as Jefe del Estado during the following thirty-five years.

In March 1945 Varela was appointed High Commission in Morocco. At his death he was made posthumously Captain General.

* * *

Yagüe was born in San Leonardo, Soria, in 1891, and died in Burgos, in 1951. He was Africanist and a Legionary in the years preceding the Civil War, and commanded the African and Legionary troops who reduced the revolutionary coup of the Asturian miners in 1934. He was an active Falangist in those years and became a friend of José Antonio.

Juan Yagüe was son of a middle class physician of Soria. He entered the Academy of Infantry of Toledo in 1907, at the same time as Francisco Franco and Emilio Esteban-Infantes (the Second Commander of the Blue Division during World War II). In 1912 he was First Lieutenant in Burgos. Two years later he was at the Saboya Regiment n.º 6 in Tetouan. In the war of Africa he combated with the Legion from its early years. In 1936 he was in command of that elite fighting force when Franco flew to Ceuta from the Canary Islands.

After 18th July 1936, once in Spain, after a complicated operation in which Legionaries and Moroccan volunteers crossed the Strait of Gibraltar, Yagüe contributed to secure Seville for the Nationalits and began immediately his incredible march towards Madrid: 14 km per day in the first four weeks. The battle of Badajoz was one of the most bloody of the first months of the war. On 14th August the Legionaries, with very heavy casualties, broke a pass through the old walls protecting the city and confronted man to man the brave Anarchist and Socialist defenders. The leftist propaganda gave then a very large number of victims of the repression. *La Voz* gave 9,000, incredible for a relative small city as Badajoz. Journalists in all over the world reported vividly the blood shed using also very large figures, 2,000 victims. A recent serious study by A.D. Martín Rubio, using the Civil Record of all deaths in the period 1936-1945 gives a maximum figure of 172 victims in August and 191 in September. Pío Moa estimates the number of men shot in Badajoz in the Summer and Fall of 1936 between 200 and 600, a very large number, but not too high comparison with those shot or assassinated after 18th July at *Cuartel de la Montaña* and *Cárcel Modelo*. It is not unlikely that Jay Allen, from the *Chicago Tribune*, reported 4,000 victims in Badajoz, *the city of the horrors*, with great international repercussion to compensate in part for the well known horror which had taken place in Madrid three weeks before, when the Government of the Republic decided to distribute arms to the revolutionary masses.

When Yagüe forces, exhausted, arrived in Maqueda, not far from Madrid, the advance had already slowed down from 14 km per day to 2.3 km per day in the previous 18 days. At that moment Franco decided to take a detour to liberate the Alcazar of Toledo, a symbol of the resistance to the overwhelming superiority of the revolutionary forces. Yagüe disagreed, and Franco decided to transfer command of the Legionaries and Regulars to Varela, who liberated those remaining under siege at the Alcazar of Toledo on 27th September 1936.

Approaching Madrid, Yagüe disagreed again with Franco. He thought it was better to attack from the North, from what is now

Plaza de Castilla instead of attacking from the South, from the Manzanares river and *Ciudad Universitaria*. But the International Brigades were already in Madrid, and after a bloody fight the combat ended up in draw.

Franco realized that a quick victory had become impossible and decided for a more cautious long term strategy.

Later, Yagüe played a decisive role at the Ebro battle in 1938, as head of the 1st Moroccan Army. After victory he entered Barcelona in January 1939 without shooting a single shot.

After the Civil War he was named Minister of the Air Force in August 1939. Disagreements with Franco resulted in his confinement in his native village of San Leonardo, Soria, on 27th June 1940. It was rumoured that he was somehow implicated at that time in a plot to enter World War II on the side of Germany.

In 1944, as Captain General of the VI Military Region (Burgos), he had a decisive role in defeating the *maquis* (former Republican combatants) which had entered Spain through the Pyrenees.

He died in Burgos in 1952. Posthumously, he was awarded the Silver Palm of the *Falange*.

FÉLIX SCHLAYER AND *PASIONARIA*

Félix Schlayer Gratwohl, consul of Norway in Madrid in 1936, was an engineer born in Reutlingen (Germany), established in Spain as *impresario* of agricultural machinery already for many years when the Civil War broke out. Norway's ambassador was abroad on 18th July 1936, and Félix Schlayer became head of Norway's legation in Madrid. In this capacity, he saved the lives of more than one thousand refugees, giving them shelter at the legation in the first months of the war. He was a true humanitarian hero who risked his life many times, during that period of extreme violence and anarchy. In November, when the decimated and exhausted forces of the Army of Africa were approaching Madrid, after liberating the Alcazar of Toledo, Largo Caballero's government decided to move to Valencia. At that time, revolutionary socialist, communist and anarchist militia, encouraged by the red government, made systematic effort to suppress the so-called *fifth column*, within the capital of Spain, which according to the republican propaganda, was ready to join the two Franco columns advancing from the South and the two Mola columns advancing from the North.

Félix Schlayer was the man who discovered and denounced the indiscriminate butchery which took place in Paracuellos del

Jarama. Between four and six thousand preventive prisoners were brought out from the jails of Madrid and murdered within a few weeks.

As my good friend José Manuel Ezpeleta says in the prologue to the translation of Schlayer's book, published by Ediciones Altera (2006), it is relatively well known that thousands of rank and file Catholics, priests and nuns were assassinated at that time in the first few months of the Spanish Civil War, because of their religious convictions. However, perhaps not so well known is the fact that, thanks to the commendable efforts of members of the diplomatic bodies established in Madrid the lives of thousands of persons were saved taking refuge in the embassies and foreign legations of the capital. This was, no doubt, a brilliant page written by a handful of diplomats, one of which was Félix Schlayer, certainly an outstanding example, moved not by ideological motives, but only by pure human solidarity.

According to José Manuel Ezpeleta, during the Spanish Civil War there were more than seven thousand the persons who received diplomatic asylum in about thirty embassies and foreign legations in Madrid. In those years there were many diplomats who had no hesitation in risking their lives in order to save the lives of those given shelter at their embassies and legations. Daniel García Mansilla, ambassador of Argentina, and Aurelio Núñez Morgado, ambassador of Chile, deserve, with Félix Schlayer, a place of honor among them.

The massive killing of innocent Spaniards in Paracuellos del Jarama, so similar to the massive killing of innocent Polish men in Katyn a few years later, is no doubt one of the darkest pages of revolutionary terror in the 20th century.

Schlayer's book registers this interchange between Schlayer and Dolores Ibárruri, *la Pasionaria*:

> Towards the end I asked *la Pasionaria* how did she imagine that the two halves of Spain, divided by such an abysmal hatred, could live as a single people (after the war) and endure each other again. She exploded furiously: «It is simply impossible! There is no other solution than one half of Spain eliminating the other!».

(Félix Schlayer, *Diplomat im Roten Madrid*, Herbig F.A., Verlagsbuchhand Lung GMBH, Munich, 1938, p. 226)

WORLD WAR AND COLD WAR

Serrano Súñer: *Rusia es culpable*

Ambassador Hayes

Plaza de Oriente, 1946

Jardiel Poncela´s Open Letter

Herbert Matthews Letter to Moscardó's widow

Eisenhower in Madrid, 1959

Nixon and Franco

Adiós, Francisco Franco, 1975

SERRANO SÚÑER: *RUSIA ES CULPABLE*

Luis Suárez, a distinguished historian and member of the Spanish Royal Academy of History, organized in 1992 a Summer Course on Francisco Franco and his epoch, coinciding with the centenary of Franco's birth year, for Universidad Complutense, Madrid. General Alonso Baquer, other various former collaborators in different governments of Franco, like José María García Escudero, Gonzalo Fernández de la Mora, Laureano López Rodó, as well as former political adversaries of Franco, like José Prat (Socialist), Marcelino Camacho (Communist) and Fernando Arrabal (Anarchist) were among the speakers at that Summer Course. In the audience was, almost one hundred years old himself but in relative good shape, don Ramón Serrano Súñer, brother-in-law of Franco and former Minister of Foreign Affairs with him in the early years of World War II.

Hitler's panzer divisions had occupied half of Poland, Holland, Belgium and most of France, after throwing into the sea the British forces at Dunkerque.

In an aside in between two lectures I had a good opportunity to approach don Ramón Serrano Súñer, in animated conversation with other participants at the Summer Course, and ask him:

- Don Ramón: I have the impression that just before the outbreak of World War II, when Franco saw that Hitler signed an agreement with Stalin to invade Catholic Poland, your brother-in-law decided not to trust Hitler any more. As co-protagonist and close collaborator of Franco at the time, would you confirm my impression or not?

Serrano looked to me smiling and said:

- Well, Franco was a rather histrionic man...

Of course, this was not a real answer to my question. It showed, only, that don Ramón, having been a most direct collaborator of his brother-in-law from the early months of the Spanish Civil War, still resented very much having been replaced as Minister of Foreign Affairs in September 1942, when Franco decided that Germany was beginning to lose the war, and that another man, more likeable to the Allies should be put in his place.

Serrano Súñer, a bright and competent man, married to a sister of doña Carmen Polo, Franco's wife, had been a member of the Spanish Cortes in the last years of the Republic. He belonged then to the right of center Christian Democratic party, CEDA, and was a good friend and admirer of José Antonio Primo de Rivera, the leader of *Falange Española*. At that time, Serrano Súñer transmitted a letter from José Antonio to Franco, and he arranged later an interview between both men. In 1937 he arrived in Salamanca, then the capital of the National Zone, having been rescued from Madrid's *Cárcel Modelo*. Two of his brothers had been killed in the Republican Zone. He was very influential in bringing up the decree of unification of the *Falange* and the Traditionalists, which formed the basis for the *Movimiento Nacional* (FET-JONS). He was soon named Minister of the Interior and became known as the *cuñadísimo* in the zone under Franco's rule. Serrano was known then as an admirer of Mussolini's Italy and Hitler's Germany. Years later he would visit Hitler and Ribbentrop in Berlin. When Hitler's panzer divisions invaded Russia on 22nd June 1941, Serrano was Minister of Foreign Affairs. This was good news for Spain, for Franco and for his Minister of Foreign Affairs. They had been able of obstructing for months Hitler's plans to invade Gibraltar and to close the Mediterranean to the British Navy at its West end. Franco, who was convinced that Spain should be kept out of the war at all costs, insisted that the East end of the Mediterranean must be closed first.

The invasion of Russia by the German panzer divisions released the pressure on Spain to enter the war. Serrano told Stohrer, then German ambassador in Madrid, that «the Spanish government had seen with great satisfaction the beginning of the fight against Bolshevist Russia» and that it had decided to send volunteers to the fight on the Russian front, «in response to the fraternal help of Germany during the civil war». This was true, of course, but, at the same time, it was also a prudent measure to placate Hitler.

Serrano addressed that day an enthusiastic crowd of Falangists from the balcony of the Palace of Santa Cruz, the Ministry of Foreign Affairs, with the words:

Rusia es culpable! (Russia is guilty!).

The Spanish force sent to Russia was the famous *Blue Division*, the first contingent of volunteers, somewhat more than 18,000 men, under the command of General Muñoz Grandes, one of the Franco's comrades in arms from the days of Morocco. Very soon, they were sent to the Eastern front battle line. A second contingent of more than 20,000 would be sent later. They fought bravely, and their services at the front were much appreciated.

A few days afterwards, the High Command of the Wehrmacht decided to withdraw their plans of military action in the Iberian Peninsula as long as the campaign in Russia was underway. Two months later an upset Hitler said to a Spanish General that he was sorry Franco had not taken the opportunity to occupy Gibraltar in the previous spring. Gibraltar, however, was still obsessing the Führer during the initial victorious phase of the Russian campaign. England, he thought, in spite of its relative weakness could still launch offensives at various points in the Western fronts. Hitler suspected that the British and Americans were planning a landing in French or Spanish Morocco. If that was the case the Germans should be ready to implement countermeasures.

In the summer of 1942 Hitler was still euphoric. His armies seemed still invincible, and he could not imagine that the tide would reverse against him before year's end, both in Russia and in North Africa. His irritation with Franco and with Serrano Súñer was considerable. In contrast to the European and American left, he saw very little similarity between Franco's regime and his National Socialism. At a dinner with his close collaborators in June 1942, he said that the Spanish government was precipitating the country into a complete disaster, blaming first the priests and the monarchists. He thought that if war were to break out again in Spain, the Falangists might well be forced to join the reds against «that garbage of clergy-monarchists». Unfortunately, he said, in Spain, there was always somebody like Serrano Súñer ready to serve the interests of the Church.

From my first encounter with him –declared Hitler–, he produced in me a sense of repulsion, in spite of the opinion of our ambassador, who, with an abysmal ignorance of the facts, had presented him to me as the most ardent germanophile.

(See e. g.: *Hitler's Table Talk* [Weidenfeld and Nicolson, 1953], p. 519, quoted in Brian Crozier, *Franco: History and Biography* [London: Eyre & Spottiswoode, 1967]).

No doubt, all sensible Spaniards, right, center, and left, should be extremely grateful to Franco, to Serrano Súñer, and to the *Blue Division*, for contributing decisively, under very difficult circumstances, to avoid the involvement of Spain in the Second World War at a critical time.

AMBASSADOR HAYES

In September 1939 Europe was at war. Franco broadcasted an appeal to the leaders of the contending nations, in whose hands, he said, a «catastrophe unparalleled in history» could be unchained[1]. They did not pay any attention, of course.

He asked then to *localize* the war. On Monday, 14th September, Franco decided that all Spanish subjects should observe strict neutrality. It is true that on 12th June 1940, after France had surrendered, two days after Mussolini entered the war, Spain moved from neutrality to *non-belligerency*, a term coined to imply that Spanish sympathies were with Germany and Italy rather than with Britain, alone at that time and almost defeated. Many years later, however, a French correspondent

---

[1] George Hills, *Franco: The Man and his Nation* (R. Hale Ltd.: London, 1967), p. 337.

asked Franco[2]: «Did you at any moment think of aligning yourself with the Axis?». His reply was: «Never». He could have been possibly tempted when in 1941 Hitler engaged in war with the Soviet Union at the other end of Europe. But he knew very well that in 1940 England was not defeated, and that it was likely that at some time in the future the U.S. would enter the war. He knew this would change completely the situation. Two things were certain: the general Spanish hostility towards Stalin's Russia, so heavily involved in the Spanish Civil War, was genuine; and the firm determination in the Spanish people to stay away from the war. At the peak of Germany's power, when Hitler was tempted to cross the Pyrenees, take Gibraltar and close the Mediterranean from the West, if the Spanish government had confronted him, Spain would have suffered, no doubt, the same fate as Czechoslovakia, Denmark, Norway, Belgium and Holland.

Spain's neutrality, on the other hand, was decisive for the final outcome of the war, as pointed out by General Jodl at Nuremberg. Spain, however, was excluded in the post war years from help by the Marshall Plan. Other nations, which did let the German armies cross their borders, were not.

Let us quote Winston Churchill in the British Parliament on 24th May 1944:

> There is no doubt that if Spain had yielded to German blandishments and pressure at that juncture (1940-41), our burden would have been much heavier. The Straits of Gibraltar would have been closed, and all access to Malta would have been cut off from the West. All the Spanish coast would have become the nesting place of German U-boats. I certainly did not feel at that time that I should like to see any of these things happen and none of them did happen.

Churchill knew well the history of Spanish War of Independence against Napoleon and he referred to it in the same speech.

In December 1941, Franco's prophecy to Hitler that he would have to fight the Americans became true[3]. And, in private,

---

[2] *Ibidem*, p. 351.

[3] *Ibidem*, p. 355.

Franco began to tell visitors his theory of the three wars: the war between the nations of Western Europe (a war of commercial interests); the war between Germany and Russia (a war of Western Civilization against Communism), and the war between U.S. and Japan (in which Japan, a pagan power, said Franco, had attacked the Philippines and the U.S. had become the defender of Spanish civilization against Asiatic barbarians). This three wars theory, according to George Hills, became a favorite subject of conversation, especially with American visitors.

In May 1942, Roosevelt sent Carlton J.H. Hayes, Professor of History at Columbia University, as U.S. Ambassador to Spain. Hayes remained in Madrid until 1945. He was cultured, urbane, and a gentleman. He was respected even by Spaniards hostile to the Allies. According to Hayes[4]:

> ... so long as almost the whole continent of Europe was at the mercy of Germany, with German armies massed near the Pyrenees and German submarines infesting the seas adjacent to Spain, he (Franco) let Hitler, and indeed the whole world, believe he was pro-Axis. Nevertheless [...] at least from the date of his dismissal of Serrano Súñer from the Foreign Ministry and from the leadership of *Falange* in 1942, General Franco guided or backed the responsible officials of his government approximating Spain's official position to the pro-allied preferences of the large majority of the Spanish people.

We summarize below the pragmatic considerations of Ambassador Hayes in *Wartime Mission in Spain* [*Misión de Guerra en España*[5]] at the end of the Second World War:

> The most extended opinion on Franco's regime in the U.S. is that his government had been imposed in Spain by Hitler and Mussolini and that, without diplomatic and economic support, it would fall down by the spontaneous action of the Spanish people... In truth, Franco's regime was indebted only in part to Italy's and Germany's aid during the Spanish Civil War. This help had been much exaggerated, while the help provided by Russia and France to the loyalists had been downplayed. The civil war was first of all a Spanish business, in which half the nation and more than half the

---

[4] Carlton J.H. Hayes, *Wartime Mission in Spain* (1945); see also *Misión de guerra en España* (EPESA: Madrid, 1946).
[5] *Ibidem* (Spanish Edition), pp. 382-92.

army supported General Franco.

But, also, as shown in this book [*Wartime Mission in Spain*] and as declared by Mr. Churchill in the House of Commons in May 1944, Franco's government was not totally pro-Axis, and gave considerable facilities to the war efforts of the Allies. The support from Spain can be favorably compared to that from other neutral countries –Switzerland, Sweden, Turkey, Portugal.

The truth is that great numbers of Spaniards do not feel exploited or tortured, and that they prefer a peaceful evolution of Franco's regime to a violent revolution and to the uncertain alternatives which would accompany it.

In America there is a curious and renewed expectation on the automatic collapse of General Franco's government... What is most curious about the matter is that what has really happened in Spain does not correspond at all with the suppositions made from outside.... The recollection of the horrors of the recent Civil War is still very much alive (in Spain), and the fear to precipitate it again is a national obsession, exception made of the communist minority.

After all, the existing regime represents that part of the Spanish people that won the war, and it would be totally unheard of that the victors in such a contest were to tell the defeated: «Sorry!; we should not have won... We want to welcome your leaders, let them do whatever they want with us». Imagine General Grant saying something like this to the Chiefs and Leaders of the Southern Confederates a few years after our own civil war!...

Many Americans would like to see the other nations modeled to their own image and likeness... to see in Spain a democratic republic... On the other hand, Soviet Russia and communists all over the world would expect that Spain becomes a soviet state, a dictatorship of the proletariat. The former British Ambassador in Madrid has said that he hopes a constitutional Monarchy of the English type is reinstated in Spain.

If I am to judge by my experience in the Peninsula I must confess that I am extremely skeptical about a happy realization of such hopes. The majority of the Spanish people is indifferent, if not hostile, to the Bourbon Monarchy... On the other hand a good number of republicans and socialists blame the communist minority no less than the rightists for the tragedy of the Civil War and at least a good part of them would be ready to make common cause with the right against a communist takeover, which, therefore, had to be imposed with foreign aid [Russian, no doubt]...

The Spaniards do not have the same political history as we have. Their two experiences with republican governments –one in 1870 and the other in 1931– were unfortunate, and did not leave any hot ashes to try again. On the other hand, dictatorship, one way or the other, is not a novelty, but an old tradition of Spanish political life, historically exercised by the left and by the right... A great number of countries of the world are governed by military dictatorship. What about Portugal? Or Turkey, or Brazil, or half a dozen Hispano-American Republics?...

The non-interference in the internal business of a foreign country is not only a personal opinion. It has been practiced since a long time and has been generally accepted by the American politicians. One of their classic expressions was that of President James Monroe in 1823... «to consider the *de facto* government as the legitimate for us: to develop friendly relationships with it, and to maintain more relationships through a frank, firm and strong policy, attending in each case to the just petitions; not tolerating any injury...».

[Spaniards] do not constitute by themselves any menace for the neighboring countries or for the peace of the world, and they are, by tradition and by temperament, inflexibly opposed to international regimentation and to foreign interference. The existing regime is considered by the majority, from the right and from the left, including General Franco, as something temporary. They are sure it will change in due time...

In spite of these pragmatic and reasonable considerations, the United Nations declared an international boycott on Spain. As George Hills notes, with this the United Nations did unite Spain behind Franco effectively for many years to come.

The nationalist armies won the Civil War with the support of the losers of the Second World War, while the republican armies (the *red* armies, as they called themselves) lost with the support of the winners of the Second World War. Contrary to leftist propaganda, which has dominated the field before, during and after the Spanish Civil War, Franco's Spain was neither *Fascist*, nor *Nazi*. Franco's government was supported, from the beginning, by a conglomerate of traditionalists (*requetés*), Falangists (*syndicalists*, rather than national-socialists), some monarchists, many disenchanted Christian democrats, and many ordinary Catholics of all political persuasions. Their common denominator was «For God and country» and they rose against the communist revolution already under way.

Regarding Spanish neutrality, so decisive at critical times for the final victory of the Allies, the testimony of General Alfred Jodl[6], Chief of Operations of the German High Command, before the Nuremberg's Tribunal, is clear:

> ... the repeated refusals of Franco to let the German armies to cross Spain to take over Gibraltar, was one of the main causes of the German defeat.

---

[6] Brian Crozier, *Franco: A Biographical History* (1967); see also *Franco, historia y biografía*, trad. Joaquin Esteban Perruca (Editorial Magisterio Español, S.A.: Madrid, 1969).

PLAZA DE ORIENTE, 1946

On 9th December 1946, the day on which the so-called Spanish Case was to be debated at the Security Council of the United Nations, Franco convoked the people of Madrid at the Plaza de Oriente to protest the intrusion of the United Nations in the internal affairs of Spain.

The people of Madrid responded. About half a million Madrilians of all classes and conditions filled the large esplanade in front of the Royal Palace. Middle aged, old and young joined soon early groups of members of young organizations, ex-combatants and syndicalists facing the Royal Palace main balcony. The memory of the civil war was still very much alive and nobody was interested in going back to it. Half Spain had fought against the other half at the beginning, and the half Spain who fought for God and country had defeated, under very precarious conditions, the other half, made up by Socialists, Communists, Anarchists and separatists, and fellow travelers. None other than the last president of the Republic, Manuel Azaña, had said at the end of the war: «Franco did not rise against the Republic; he rose against the rabble which had seized it». Similar demonstrations took place in other Spanish cities. General Queipo de Llano, distanced from Franco for some time, addressed a large crowd in Seville asking them to stand together with the government against the foreign intrusion.

Amongst those present at the Plaza de Oriente were Gregorio Marañón, famous physician and author, one of the three original undersigners of the manifesto that called for the Republic in 1931; Jacinto Benavente, winner of the Nobel Prize for Literature, and many other distinguished academicians, and intellectuals who, in principle, were no enthusiasts of Franco's regime.

As a consequence of the resolution of the United Nations, Spain was excluded from the Marshall Plan and from the American aid to post-war ruined Europe which, fortunately, within a few years, brought up the German *miracle* and the Italian *miracle*, among others. Only in the decade of the 1960's, ten years after, would the joint Spanish-American military bases, would help to bring up a modest economic Spanish *miracle*.

According to the German historian Günther Dahm, if the United Nations had intended to strengthen Franco's government, its resolution requesting the withdrawal of ambassadors from Spain could not have been more on target. Spaniards are known to be able of criticizing ferociously their government, but they often react with indignation when foreigners do it.

According to the British author George Hills, if the Spanish Chief of government had been excommunicated by the Pope, he might feel in seriously danger, but a formal condemnation by the United Nations would lack moral weight for the large majority of Spaniards.

When Franco approached the main balcony of the Royal Palace to address the multitude, cries of «Viva España!» and «Arriba España!» greeted him, together with insults to the United Nations. In his address, Franco reminded the people that «twelve European nations» were already under Communist domination, imposed by Stalin under the cover of the agreements of Yalta and Potsdam. He reminded his listeners of the revolutionary terror in Madrid, only a few years before, and he assured them that the foreign ambassadors would eventually come back.

The figure of half a million demonstrators filling to capacity the Plaza de Oriente, authenticated by photos, with Madrid's Royal Theater in the background, is really impressive for a city like Madrid, which, at the time, had a population of no more than one and a half million inhabitants.

Franco's words were eloquent:

> We Spaniards should not be surprised at what happened in the United Nations Organization, after a wave of communist terror which is devastating Europe, and a series of violations, crimes and persecution, similar to the one you saw or suffered yourselves, has been unleashed on twelve nations till yesterday independent... it is not surprising that the sons of Giral and *Pasionaria* find support in the official representatives of those unfortunate peoples.
>
> The peaceful spirit of Spain has been sufficiently demonstrated. Her interests are not in conflict with the honest interests of the other countries. Our country serves its best interest the same way other countries serve theirs. In the same way that they defend and administer their peace, we want to administer and defend our victory.
>
> [...]
>
> As long as the world concert of nations rests on the mutual respect for the sovereignty of the peoples, nobody –except if some kind of international fascism dictates and unifies its arbitrary decisions– has a right to meddle in the private business of other nations.

From my home, at Pavía street facing the Plaza de Oriente, I remember the festive tone of the crowd protesting the *intolerable* decision of the United Nations. I was then ten years old, and my brothers nine, eight, seven and five, respectively. We were amused and slightly surprised to see a young man carrying a poster which said: «I shit myself on the U.N.». Not polite, but certainly very expressive.

JARDIEL PONCELA'S OPEN LETTER

Enrique Jardiel Poncela (1901-1952) was one of the most original and successful Spanish playwrights of the last century.

Two years after the end of World War II, he wrote an open letter to a Mexican journalist (De María y Campos), which captures very well what was really at stake in the Spanish Civil War.

Madrid, 28th May, 1947.

My good friend and dear fellow: After receiving your letter I hurry to answer you...

... In the last years political animosity and misinformation have made 100,000 miles wider the ocean which separates the seashores of Mexico and Spain.

I have never been a man of the *right* or of the *left* (referring always to the Spanish *right* and *left*). I always liked some ideas inherent to both sides, and my eclectic way of thinking was made up with that mixture...

From 1931 to 1936 the republican government –and this is the rigorous truth, most objectively and coldly considered– did not do anything useful and did much harmful […]. The indubitable reason: this republican governments did not care at all for Spain, or at least they acted as if Spain did not matter…

Such a state of decomposition, disorder, delinquency, libertinage, social hate and ruin, was the result of the government work those five years: and anybody who does not recognize it having witnessed it –my dear friend De María y Campos– be he Spaniard or foreigner lies, lies, lies…; and I have not said *lies* enough times to express how much and in which way he lies…

I defined myself not positively but negatively. I did not say to myself: I am that […]. I felt myself anti-leftist of the Spanish left only. And this only because of pure patriotism; because of pure and exclusive love of Spain…

And I defined myself in such a radical way because things had gone so far that any distinction of fine shades was already totally out of place: even in politics; the chiaroscuro was not possible; the relative was not possible; no gradation was possible any longer…

And now, my dear friend and fellow, I continue with Spain's history… and let me I begin with the basic facts as they actually took place…

When the news [of Calvo Sotelo's assassination] became known the following day throughout Spain, an impressive silence followed. When the government suspended the only two dailies which gave the full news –*El Debate* and *La Época*– and closed up the Parliament to avoid talking about it officially […] a wave of indignation, silent but virulently hot went all over Spain, North to South, East to West…

Any non-Marxist (neutral) citizen in Spain was afraid for his life. And every non-Marxist (neutral) Spaniard thought and said resolutely:

«Up to here *have* they come!».

God, they would come much further… and very soon…

This way we arrive at 17th July 1936, the day in which at 5 pm, the Army of Africa rose up, resolved to put an end to an intolerable situation which was strangling Spain. And on the 18th and the 19th all garrisons in the peninsula rose up, with street fighting, resulting in triumph in some provinces, and defeat suffocated in blood, in others.

At the time newspapers and radio were telling lies saying that the uprising had already been completely defeated, and in the mean time the Government was distributing arms among the Marxist organization in Madrid, Barcelona and the remaining cities where the uprising had been defeated... and if that was not enough, the Government opened the jails of those cities to the common prisoners... inciting them to kill.

This is the truth, all the truth, and nothing but the truth.

In summary, excepting the Marxists and their more or less sincere sympathizers, *in the loyalist territory only those who were able to hide or take refuge in a foreign embassy –and not all of them– save their life.*

But let us stop for the moments with these horror and let us go to the facts of war themselves, which you perhaps do not know and you deserve to know.

By the 19th July, Franco's Spain –nationalist Spain–counted with 26 incomplete provinces, as against 24 complete provinces (and the remnants of those incomplete) which were in the hands of the Marxists or *reds*: that way should be called the ones and the others if we want to be just and rigorous. The red territory was much larger than the nationalist, and infinitely richer in industries and mineral resources. The nationalist territory was richer, on the other hand, in livestock and agricultural resources...

Starting differences between both sides which resulted in clear benefit to the nationalists:

1st Difference

The nationalists very quickly controlled their provinces and there was still street fighting at most for ten or twelve days in some of them, which were Seville, Granada, Majorca and Saragossa. After these ten to twelve days, at most, the *nationalists* had guaranteed order in the interior and were capable of paying attention to all urgent aspects of the campaign underway, fabrication of ammunition and materials, etc. The reds, on the contrary, as I said, devoted themselves to going ahead with the revolution in their territory, stealing, killing, chasing *fascists*, and destroying: they were more interested in the communist revolution than by the war, specially in the first months; till the Communist Party (Negrín's Government) began to govern *de facto* and in full autocracy.

2nd Difference

The nationalists were from the first moment united (the discrepancies between falangists and traditionalists did not surface till 1937, were small, did not affect order and concluded with their fusion under Franco's authority...). In the meantime, the reds, albeit united in their Marxism, were disunited at heart and hostile to each other: communists and socialists against anarcho-syndicalists. This hostility became hatred: more intense as Franco's victory was becoming more likely and their own defeat was becoming more apparent. The anarchists and anarcho-syndicalists (CNT and FAI) were very numerous and very brave... and they were furiously anti-communist (Spaniard: individualist, don't ever forget...). The communists had to do battle on them: and they did –May, 1937– six days of fighting in the streets of Barcelona, with tanks and even with troops brought from the battle line of Aragon (I was in Barcelona and I saw *that* also). The communists-socialists (Negrín's Government) won, and for many nights and nights the victors made a secret but tremendous *clean up* of the defeated (by *cleaning up*, you must understand *killing*). (The defeated and decimated anarchist never did forget and took revenge on the communists by giving them the same medicine in the streets of Madrid when the war was almost finished –March, 1939– in the so-called *Communist Week*, with Franco's soldiers themselves almost ready to enter Madrid, and in those weeks the communists fell down in large quantities under the merciless attack of the anarcho-syndicalists). Single *anarchists* who fought on their own, had been murdered before by the communists; for instance, Durruti. Those deaths, of course, were presented as campaign accidents, casualties facing enemies, etc. And red soldiers believed it. Another enemy who was quashed by the communists was the POUM, a Trotskyist party. The Trotstkyists were few and once its leader, Nin, was assassinated, the party dissolved itself into the Stalinist-communist party during Negrín's Government. But, even under the ironclad dominion of that communist party, the so-called *loyalists* were the whole war divided among themselves in front of the united and better organized soldiers of Franco.

3rd Difference
The nationalists accepted right away discipline, hierarchy of command, confidence and faith in their leaders, as well as a coordinated and joint action in combat. On the contrary, the reds (to whom anti-militarism had been inculcated for years, producing contempt and hatred towards anything military...) rejected from the first moment discipline; suspected any command personified by an army officer, and –specially the first three or four months– disobeyed their chiefs and assassinated many of them, blaming all misfortunes of the war on treason by the own chiefs. All coordination and concerted action in combat was repugnant to them because their anarchist (individualistic) spirit and it was very

difficult to convince those men –persuaded as they were in one thousand meetings of how much infamous was the Army– that to suppress the Army it was necessary first to built up an army.

4th Difference

The nationalists had from the first moment spiritual and patriotic ideals for which to fight: the fatherland; the old flag, red and gold (which reminded everybody of the past); family, home, affections from youth and childhood, etc., and their religion (the Virgin of..., the Christ of...). On the contrary, the reds had no ideals, only ideas to fight for; and while the fanaticism for an idea is enough to kill, it is not enough to die for. And besides, those ideas were foreign. The Marxists, at the beginning, did not feel the foreign character of communism, but when they had to begin obeying foreign leaders, who did not know how to say hello in Spanish, and who showed themselves terribly cruel in implanting discipline –Kleber, Walter, Hans, Douglas, Torunczyk, Gorieff, Luckas, Morandi, Dumas, Kopik–, they felt that that idea for which they were fighting was not theirs, and then something rebelled within themselves as Spaniards, in spite of their fanaticism. The red Government noticed that dangerous reaction and tried to ensure, always within their possibilities, that the foreigner leaders in the war had in their staffs transmitting orders secondary Spanish leaders –Líster, *Campesino*, Mera, Modesto Guilloto, Tagueña, etc.–, some of whom came to be true leaders because their instinctive natural talents, not rare in Spain, a country and a race of individualists (e.g., Cipriano Mera, anarchist, brickmason, who became a true leader, to be taken seriously into consideration when leading men in action; he was the one who, commanding his men, defeated the communists in March 1939). In any case, in 1938, in general, the red combatants had lost most of their faith in communism, and were fighting more by fear of the enemy and by mere inertia than by those ideas about which they were already disillusioned.

5th Difference

In the nationalist camp regarding war the events of the war, truth was said always unadorned, when it was going well, when it was going half well, and the few times it was going bad. *The Official Report of the War* from Salamanca was the Gospel regarding veracity and accuracy; and was this way always. With such veracity –confirmed a thousand times– the rearguard and, specially, the nationalist combatants saw strengthened their faith in Franco, their admiration and their respect; their gratitude for the faith he had in his Army and in his rearguard; and, on the other hand, the nationalist rearguard and Army felt growing, day by day, growing the distrust, the contempt, the scorn and the disgust towards the red cause, which lied always systematically. The *Red Official Report* never told the truth on the train of events in the war; it feigned red victories and nationalist defeats which had never existed; it hid its crimes and attributed them to the enemy; and these constant lies, regularly confirmed, ended up by being the gossip in their rearguard and even in their Army itself. I heard in Barcelona convinced Marxists saying: «Well, tonight we will know the truth in the *rebel's* broadcasts». Not confessed, but generally felt, the rearguard and the red Army ended up believing more the nationalist *official report* than their own.

6th Difference

The nationalists had abundant and cheap food all throughout the war, and the reds only in a small minority ate abundantly and cheaply. In the rearguard there was soon scarcity, very soon in seventy percent of the homes. This was because the reds, from 18th July on, stole and robbed establishments; sacked stores; killed the livestock; interrupted the agricultural activities, and administered foolishly the little that was left. To achieve an abundance which the reds refused to believe, Franco simply had administered well a territory which had not been sacked, and where the livestock had not been shot, a territory in which sowing and recollection went forward not only as usual but intensified. Because of this, Franco had food for his territory and for the conquered territories, food enough to throw sacks of bread over hungry Madrid by plane, in small parachutes; the reds, furious, said the bread had been poisoned, and shot those who tried to pick up the sacks. Of course, no one believed the tale of the *poisoning*.

7th Difference

From the first day to the end of the war the nationalists always had a spirit of sacrifice. The reds never had it. Because the ones fought for the spiritual and the others for the material; the first knew how to renounce everything in order to win, while the others renounced winning in order to have anything. (A man dispossessed from his property fights to recover it. A man who keeps property which is not his property, wants only to enjoy the product of his robbery). Indalecio Prieto summarized in an aphorism this great truth that contributed so much to Franco's success: the rich learned to be poor and the poor did not learn to be rich.

8th Difference

The nationalist Army from the first day got used to going forward and attacking. On the other hand, the red Army soon became used to defending itself and retreating. «They won't overcome!», cried the reds always, to the great applause of the stupid world opinion in general. But, if the general opinion of the world –and of the reds– would have not been so stupid, they would have said: «We will overcome!», which would have meant success.

9th Difference

Above all the lies and the propaganda, past and present, in the national camp there were much less, infinitely less, overwhelmingly less foreign combatants than in the red camp[7] [...]. The nationalists accustomed themselves from the beginning to count on their own forces, and this strengthened them. On the other hand, the reds, up to the last moment, accustomed themselves to expect from abroad a decisive help (foreign intervention, world war, etc.), and this softened them.

10th Difference

The nationalists always had evident examples of the heroism of their own: defense of the Alcazar of Toledo; defense of the Sanctuary of *Santa María de la Cabeza*; defense of Belchite and Quinto; defense of Oviedo; defense of the Barracks of Simancas, etc., etc. The reds had no such heroic examples in their own camp. So the nationalists knew they had heroic examples and they were conscious of their obligation to be worthy of them The others lacked that tremendous resource.

11th Difference

The nationalists never hated the reds. (It astonished me to arrive in 1938 at the *nationalist* zone and see this lack of any hatred to an enemy who hated them so much. While in the *red zone*, the nationalists were always named among insults, in the *nationalist zone* they always spoke of the reds with the appellative of *rojillos* [diminutive] –extending to both: rearguard and combatants– and this, even difficult to believe, as so many things which were true,

---

[7] Jardiel Poncela probably exaggerates here. See, for instance, updated figures in Ramón Salas Larrazábal, *Los datos exactos de la Guerra Civil* (Madrid, 1980).

was said with a kind of *sympathetic commiseration* rather than with *contempt*).

Because of that, life in Spain was possible after the victory of the nationalists: because there was no hatred from the nationalists to the Marxists. *Even if the propaganda says the contrary.* The propaganda lies and it has lied *always*. On the contrary, the Marxist hatred of the nationalists was such that, in the case of a Marxist victory, the end of the war would have been an apocalyptic catastrophe of hundreds of thousands of victims. You must be sure it would, my friend. And this right away, only few hours only after victory and even before the full sovietization of Spain, which would have followed immediately that victory. And then...

12th and last Difference

Because the war was preceded by the five years of calamitous republican government, as described already, which had disappointed talented men of the left (like: Unamuno, Ortega y Gasset, Marañón, Baroja, etc.) in 1936, at the beginning of the war, *almost* all *select* Spaniards were on the side of the nationalists –or in spirit with them at least–. One month after the beginning of the war and in view of the Marxist crimes, this had become *almost* a *totality*. On the side of the Marxists –or in spirit with them– were only the mediocre, the frankly inferior, the hopelessly fanatic and those who had compromised themselves to such an extent that they could not go back. In a civil war this phenomenon is all-important. Because if the totality, or *almost* totality of the *select* leans to one side, facing it lines up only the remnant after the selection; in other words, the less select component of the country, the mental scum, to which nothing select can be attributed. And I have no need to tell you how much the mental category (in all order of things, social and professional) is determinant in a war. It simply determines victory. And this law was once more fulfilled ...

Mexico and Spain had no diplomatic relations at that time. And many republican exiles chose Mexico, with its left-leaning PRI (*Partido Revolucionario Institucionalista*) in power, as their new home, including Indalecio Prieto. However, in spite of this, during those years the movies of Jorge Negrete and María Félix, of Pedro Armendáriz and Dolores del Río, were extremely popular in Spain. No wonder. For centuries, before its independence, Mexico had been called *Nueva España*, in the same way the present State of Massachusetts is still called New

England. When Agustín Lara, the great Mexican composer, author of the *chotis Madrid* visited the capital of Spain, he was received extremely well.

More or less at that time, the time Jardiel Poncela and De María were interchanging letters across the Atlantic, rumors circulated in Madrid that when Manolete, the greatest Spanish bullfighter, entered into Mexico's D.C. bullring, he saw, and was somewhat surprised, that side by side with the Mexican flag was in the place of honor the flag of the Spanish Republic. According to those rumors, he quietly returned inside and told the accompanying local authority: *Yo no toreo con ese trapo!* (I don't perform with that rag!). I have been unable of confirming the rumor but I was told that Manolete fought with the nationalists in the Civil War and that he refused to shake his hand with Prieto in Mexico.

Manolete was, no question, the most admired and famous Spanish bullfighter of the 20th century, and Arruza was his most famous Mexican contemporary counterpart.

Manolete was killed by a bull at the bullring of Linares, in Andalusia, not long after he visited Mexico D.C. He has never been forgotten by the *aficionados* in Spain.

* * *

It is quite interesting, I think, to examine the long term shifts in Spanish *public opinion* along the last eighty years or so.

After the Civil War, and specially during the World War years, which the country so miraculously managed to escape, and even later, during most of the Cold War years, up to 1975, I think Jardiel Poncela's description of our civil war probably was a fairly accurate description of the main line *public opinion* in Spain.

From 1975 to 1978 however, a smooth *democratic* transition began to take place under the monarchy re-installed by Franco. That *transition* took place, it should be recalled, under such slogans as «We only reform what we want to conserve». But, gradually, within a few years, a drastic change in *public opinion* took place orchestrated by *centrists*, socialists, communists and separatists, heirs of those whose behavior during the years of the republic and the civil war had almost ruined the country. But also –and this is most striking– with the benevolent acquiescence of the rightist leaders, now disguised as centrists. Jardiel, who was not by his own admission a man of the right, probably would have found shocking what passes today for *current public opinion* on the Civil War.

For the first time, World opinion regarding the nationalists is now somewhat better regarding the Civil War than Spanish opinion. This proves only one thing: that public opinion can be easily manipulated. Hopefully not for ever.

HERBERT MATTHEWS LETTER

The heroic defense of the Alcazar of Toledo by Colonel Moscardó and his men from July to September 1936 had a tremendous impact on the world public opinion. Up to the moment of the Alcazar's liberation, public opinion took for granted that the military-civic rising against the Republican government, already controlled by the revolutionaries (communists, anarchists and fellow travelers), was doomed to fail. Only after the miraculous liberation of the Alcazar by the nationalists did world public opinion begin to take seriously into consideration the possibility that the rebels could win.

The liberation of the Alcazar was one of those events which the republican radio and the newspapers desperately tried to hide from the Marxist masses. The account of Jardiel Poncela, at the time in Madrid, is as follows:

But in the Government inner circles (the Alcazar stubborn resistance) had produced a crisis, hidden for the moment. No wonder. Leaving aside the stubborn fierce heroism inspired by (then) colonel Moscardó, of the defenders of the Alcazar (with 800 women and children inside!); and leaving aside also the impetuous heroism, no less stubborn, of those scarcely 4,000 men –the best of Franco's army– who did not cease advancing north fighting in the open fields (under the terrible heat of the Spanish summer, in Extremadura and La Mancha); discounting those important factors, Toledo was lost to the reds due to the obstinate and fanatical brutality of Largo Caballero, who, obsessed by the bloody vengeance he wanted to inflict on the brave, one hundred percent Spaniards defending themselves among ruins, kept up to the last moment 10,000 men surrounding the Alcazar! When with two thousand it would have been more than sufficient to keep the siege, and sending the remaining 8,000 over against the advancing nationalists, who arrived fatigued and exhausted, he would have obtained the two objectives in his dream: the final defeat of those advancing to the rescue of the Alcazar, and the final sacrifice of the Alcazar itself. Providence and the nature of things blinded that man, already blind himself; but that blindness could not be forgiven by Moscow which was the director of the orchestra. And from that moment was decreed the political death of the Spanish Lenin, who never knew how to be Lenin and never knew how to be Spanish. The materialization of his political death was delayed, but it was decreed that day; and from there on the Socialist Party would be under the orders of Indalecio Prieto, although having lost already in the communist mass its significance and its name as a party...

Twenty years later, in 1957, a distinguished American journalist, Herbert L. Matthews, member of the Editorial Board of the *New York Times* published *The Yoke and the Arrows. A Report on Spain* (George Braziller Incs: New York, 1957). A book heavily biased on the Spanish Civil War.

In this book Matthews embarked himself in an ambitious operation to dismantle once and for all the *myth* of the Alcazar of Toledo. Based upon the testimony of two former red combatants, Luis Quintanilla and José Asensio, by then both U.S. citizens, Matthews wrote that it might be a pity to demolish such a marvelous legend as that of the Alcazar; but, he said he History would demolish it anyway, as it did with the myth of George Washington and the cherry tree.

Matthews flatly denies in his book that the telephone conversation of colonel Moscardó with his son Luis during the Alcazar's siege had ever taken place.

A conclusive answer came forward soon from the pen of Manuel Aznar, a prestigious Spanish journalist and author, who made a point by point refutation of Matthews' thesis in *El Alcázar no se Rinde* (recently reissued by Espasa Calpe: Madrid, 2006, together with the Spanish translation of *The Yoke and the Arrows*).

According to Aznar, Matthews makes three statements that are three serious errors. The truth is that:

1. Colonel Moscardó's name was not Juan, but José...
2. Colonel Moscardó was never nominal chief of the Alcazar, but effective chief...
3. The telephone call received in the Alcazar on 23rd July 1936 did not come from Madrid, but from Toledo...

Apparently, Matthews' denial of any conversation between colonel Moscardó and his son (believing the account of his two republican informants), does not take into account who was in control at that time of the central telephone service in Toledo, and, therefore, who was able to open, close and re-open telephone contact at any time. When Matthews describes as a case of «incredible simplicity and stupidity» the account of Moscardó's telephone conversation with his son, he does not seem to be aware of the many cases of political simplicity and foolishness afforded by red propaganda from 1931 to 1936.

Fortunately, the incontrovertible arguments of Aznar made Matthews recant. Some time thereafter, the New York journalist wrote to doña María Guzmán de Moscardó, general Moscardó's widow, apologizing for *having been quite wrong* on the issue. Ángel Palomino, in his *Defensa del Alcázar* (Planeta: Barcelona, 1998), reproduces a photocopy of Matthews' letter to Moscardó's widow:

The New York Times
Time Square, New York 36
September, 20, 1960

Señora Doña Guzmán de Moscardó:
My dear Señora de Moscardó:
I am writing to you at the suggestion of a friend of mine, who tells me that the passage in my book called *The Yoke & the Arrows* concerning the Alcazar caused pain to you and your family. This I regret very much, and I ask you and your family to accept my sincerest apologies.

I am sure you all realize that I wrote what I did in the original version in good faith. I believe also that those who furnished me with that information, likewise did so in good faith.

However, I have become convinced after reading the evidence published by Manuel Aznar and after discussing the matter with other people to whom I trust, that I must have been entirely mistaken.

I am preparing a revised edition of my book to be published next year, and I can assure you that the passage on the Alcazar will not appear in it.

If you so desire, I would have no objection whatever to you giving whatever publicity you think fit to this letter.

Sincerely yours,
Herbert L. Matthews
Editorial Board
HLM/gm

Two things are clear from this letter: first, that Herbert L. Matthews was so carried away by his left-leaning sympathies that it resulted in a very distorted view of events at the Spanish Civil War; and second, that he was honest enough to recognize his error in this particular case, something not very common in the left or in the right, for that matter.

In a recent book by Inocencio (Chencho) Arias, former Spanish Ambassador in the U.N., entitled *Los Presidentes y la Diplomacia* (Madrid, 2012), an anecdote about Ronald Reagan and Moscardó shows strikingly how ignorant and insensitive were both ambassador Arias and the Spanish Minister of Foreign Affairs, Pérez Llorca, in July 1981, when they were officially received by the American President in Washington.

In 1981, being Leonid Brezhnev *supreme czar* in Soviet Russia, three events took place in quick succession. At that time Russia was still one of the two world superpowers. In March there had been an attempt on the life of Ronald Reagan just weeks after he had assumed office as first term president at the White House. A few days before, on 23rd February, there took place the frustrated *coup d'état* in Madrid, originally planned, it seems with the king's support, to result in a coalition government (left, center and right). Finally, on 13th May, there was the criminal attempt on the life of Pope John Paul II, at Saint Peter's Square. Ali Agca, whose links with the Bulgarian government, and therefore, with the KGB had triggered the gun.

President Reagan was determined from the very beginning to confront decisively Soviet Communism, but he knew he must do it smoothly, indirectly, to avoid the outcry of leftist propaganda. He knew perfectly well that nationalist Spain had inflicted the first important defeat on Soviet Communism in the civil war. And he knew, also, like any well informed high ranking politician of his age and time, that the defense of the Alcazar had had a tremendous world resonance in 1936. Of course, he also knew that Franco's Spain had been a most important ally of the U.S. in the Cold War against the Soviets.

The humorous commentaries of ambassador Arias on Reagan, the *Emperor* (in Arias words), and inventor of the *War of the Galaxies*, as well as his surprise at Reagan's insistence in bringing up Moscardó and the Alcazar of Toledo into the conversation are certainly out of place.

Some years after 1981, when Reagan met Gorbachev at Helsinki to discuss war and peace issues, Professor Trepakov, a physicist from Leningrad, was visiting professor for a few months at my department in the *Universidad Autónoma de Madrid*. One day I brought him in my car from the University to home, near Gran Via. Somehow the Helsinki *peace* talks came up in the conversation. Reagan and Gorbachev were the protagonists. Trepakov asked me during the ride what I thought about the peace talks. I said that it seemed reasonable to me that when two strong men are confronting each other with a sword in one hand, both should be glad to have a shield in the other. Professor Trepakov began pouring insults upon the imperialist

Americans... until I interrupted him: «Tell me, is it true or not that Patriarch Pimen, the head of the Russian Orthodox Church, is in the payroll of the KGB?». Trepakov shut up for a moment and then said more peacefully: «No, Patriarch Pimen is a very old man ... His second in command, yes, he belongs to the KGB».

End of the political discussion.

EISENHOWER IN MADRID, 1959

Vernon Walters was a United States Army officer and diplomat who served with distinction under five Presidents (Truman, Eisenhower, Johnson, Nixon and Ford) and later became Deputy Director of the CIA, and finally Ambassador to the U.N. under Nixon. He was fluent in French, Italian, Spanish, Portuguese and German. He appears between General Eisenhower and General Franco in the most publicized photo of Eisenhower's visit to Madrid in 1959 with occasion of the farewell of the two heads of state (see Vernon A. Walters, *Silent Missions*: Doubleday, New York, 1978).

It is appropriate to reproduce here his words about the stop in Madrid of Eisenhower on the occasion of the long trip to Europe and Asia. When he saw that, as scheduled originally, Eisenhower was flying from France to Morocco, he said to Press Secretary, Jim Haggerty: «You mean we are over-flying Spain, which is letting us keep our bases, and going to Morocco, which is asking us to leave?». Haggerty replied: «But Spain is a dictatorship». I answered: «What do you think a lot of countries we are visiting are?». Finally, Madrid was included in the schedule, and produced a crowd second in size only to that of New Delhi.

His summary in *Silent Missions* of the visit to the Spanish capital goes as follows:

The next stop was the Spanish capital, Madrid, an hour and a half away. Here again my services would be required. At Torrejón Air Base, Franco read a warm speech of welcome to the President as we stood on a little dais, and I whispered a running translation to the President. Then (Eisenhower) spoke and I repeated the speech in Spanish. Ten years later I was to translate a speech by President Nixon at the same place, and the Spanish Radio gave me (as a compliment) a cassette with my translation of President Eisenhower's speech in 1959 and President Nixon's in 1969. The crowds in Madrid were very large and their welcome extraordinarily enthusiastic. I rode in the car with the President and Franco and I can only report that there were a lot of «Viva Franco» shouts. The visible popularity of the man regarded by many as a hated dictator was not reflected in the press accounts of the visit. Eisenhower, however, was much impressed by this and the way Franco moved through large crowds.

President Eisenhower had struck just the right note at the airport with the Spaniards by asking how he could feel a stranger in Spain. He came from a country that had states called California, Colorado, Florida, Nevada, Texas and Arizona. Later the traffic circle outside the airport was renamed *Glorieta Eisenhower*. I could not help but contrast this with the tiny street with no buildings on it which bears his name in Paris –a city liberated by his armies–. Human gratitude is fickle.

That night Franco gave a state dinner for the President at the Oriente Palace, where the Kings of Spain had lived, but which Franco preferred not to occupy himself. He lived at the spacious but much smaller palace of El Pardo a few miles out of town. When Napoleon had installed his brother, Joseph, as King of Spain in this Palacio de Oriente, he had said to him: «Now, Joseph, you will be better housed than I am». There were warm toasts at the dinner and following it there was a short concert by five violinists all playing Stradivarius violins –priceless treasures in their hands.

The next morning, 22nd December, I rode with the President out to El Pardo for the meetings with Franco. This started with a breakfast which was so good-humored and relaxed that Eisenhower asked me to tell General Franco a story which I had previously told Ike and which had greatly amused him. The story went like this:

In Napoleon's army there was a colonel named Dupont. He was extraordinarily brave, which is frequent among colonels, and extraordinarily stupid, which is very rare among colonels. But he was crazy to become a general, which is universal among colonels. Napoleon said that he knew Dupont was brave but he simply could not have a general that stupid in the French Army. However, at the Battle of Austerlitz Napoleon saw Dupont charging at the head of the cavalry of the Guard, cutting down the Russians and the Austrians and practically winning the battle. As he watched he saw Dupont stagger and fall from his horse. He had been hit. Much moved, Napoleon dispatched his aide and his surgeon Larrey to see what Larrey could do for Dupont. Not long afterward, the young aide came riding back to Napoleon and said: «Sire, Colonel Dupont has been shot through the head. The bullet went in one ear and came out the other. Larrey says he is still conscious, but will be dead before nightfall». Napoleon thought about it a moment and then said: «Dead before nightfall. Well, go down there and tell him I have just promoted him to general». The young aide dashed off and rode back to the medical tent, where Larrey was treating the new general. Larrey had given Dupont a good slug of brandy and had then sawed off the top of his skull and placed it on the table. The brain was badly damaged and Larrey was trying to put it together again when the aide burst into the tent and announced: «The Emperor Napoleon has just promoted Colonel Dupont to the rank of general». Dupont had been powerfully slugged with Napoleon brandy, his brain was on the table, but through the brandy fumes he heard the magic word general, staggered to his feet, put the top of his skull back in place and tottered toward the door of the tent. Larrey ran after him saying: «Mon général, you can't leave like that. Your brain is still here on the table». «To hell with that», replied Dupont groggily, «now that I am a general I don't need it anymore».

There was much laughter from all present —some of whom were generals—. Franco joined in and then commented slyly to Eisenhower: «Did you notice how much harder those who are not generals laughed?». I had not suspected Franco of this kind of humor. Then he said: «The reason why generals are as bad as they are is because they are chosen from among the best colonels». At this the generals present really laughed. Later we went into Franco's study. There was a brief discussion of the U.S. bases. Franco felt that his economic situation was improving and it would not be many years before Spain became a prosperous country like the other nations of Europe and this indeed did happen. Then

Eisenhower asked him for his assessment of the intentions of the Soviets. Franco, speaking calmly, gave a most detached and unemotional appraisal of what they were trying to do. Namely, stay out of a major war but press everywhere and when anything was yielded they would press on. If they encountered serious resistance, they would press somewhere else. He did predict that the Soviets would try by all means to destroy the Western nations' will to resist and the conviction that they had something worth defending. In this too he proved a good prophet. I was to see him many years later in this same room to discuss what would happen to Spain following his death. He was to be just as unemotional and detached in discussing this event.

We took off from El Pardo in a helicopter and flew to the Torrejón Air Base. Franco showed no emotion as the helicopter lifted off and I was astonished a few minutes later when in reply to a question by Eisenhower as to whether he used helicopters much, the Spanish leader replied that he had never flown in a helicopter before. One would never have guessed it from his composure. He and Eisenhower embraced warmly at the airport and Ike boarded his plane. I sat in the fairly large cabin in the rear of the plane. I had a window seat and watched the Spaniards and Americans waving goodbye as the plane taxied slowly away. I said: «I can read lips and I can tell what they are all saying». Others aboard the plane nibbled at the bait and asked: «What are they saying?». I answered: «It's extraordinary— they are all saying the same thing». «What is that?», everyone wanted to know. I replied: «They are all saying, "Thank God they're gone!"». This got a good laugh and was probably very close to the real truth. For the host country as for the U.S. Embassy in that country, a presidential visit is an exhausting and shattering experience.

NIXON AND FRANCO

President Nixon told Vernon Walters that he wanted to see him one day in February 1971. Nixon told Walters that he had been reflecting about the situation in Spain and about what might happen there after Franco's death. Spain was vital for the West and he did not want to see any chaotic or anarchic situation to develop. The President said that he wanted Walters to go to Spain and see Franco alone, if he could, and find out what he had in mind concerning events after his own demise.

In what follows there is a concise summary of the *silent mission* to Madrid in order to see and talk to Franco. Nixon gave Walters a letter for General Franco and told him to deliver it personally. Finally, the President told Walters that if he felt it necessary, Nixon himself would tell Ambassador Robert Hill in Madrid about the matter, but that Walters should not let him get involved in order to avoid problems with the Spanish Foreign Office.

In what follows, the silent mission is narrated in Walters' own words:

I flew to Madrid on 23rd February and gave Ambassador Hill the letter addressed to him. Even though that letter did not refer to the purpose of my visit, Ambassador Hill, a shrewd and able diplomat, guessed at once what had brought me to Madrid. He was not like many of his colleagues who believe that there should be no contact with the chief of state in the country where they are accredited except through them. This parochial point of view has been a problem on many occasions. These men forget that they are the President's representative and he may conduct foreign policy through whatever channels he chooses. Ambassador Hill believed that it would be difficult to arrange a meeting with Franco as Foreign Minister Gregorio López Bravo was out of the country. I said that I felt confident I could arrange this through Chief of Government Admiral Luis Carrero Blanco. I knew him quite well and felt sure that he would help me. On the following day, I saw Admiral Carrero Blanco in his office alone and told him that I had been instructed by President Nixon to seek an audience with General Franco alone. I also told him that I had a letter from the President with instructions to hand it to the generalissimo. Carrero Blanco asked me if this matter had been taken up through any of the ministries and I said that I did not believe that it had. He then said that he would see Franco at 1 pm the following day and would discuss the matter with him.

Later that evening Ambassador Hill asked me to come over and see him. He said that on his return from Tunisia, López Bravo had been notified by Carrero Blanco of the request. At this time, López Bravo was reported to be involved in some difficulties. He was later exonerated but that evening he was quite agitated and had asked Ambassador Hill to come over and see him the next morning. I felt it was very important that Ambassador Hill's position be protected and suggested that he tell López Bravo that I had arrived in the country with a letter from the President. Since the Foreign Minister was out of the country and there was a certain urgency to the matter, I had not wished to go through the acting Foreign Minister and I had telephoned Admiral Carrero Blanco, whom I knew personally, and who was the next higher authority in the government. Ambassador Hill agreed to this and by the time he saw the Foreign Minister the next morning, López Bravo was quite relaxed but still very curious about the nature of my mission. The Foreign Minister asked if I would come over and see him, as he had known me since 1959. I agreed to see him and went to the Foreign Ministry, where he received me alone. I explained the circumstances of my visit, but did not discuss the nature of my message, nor did I tell him what I was attempting to ascertain from General Franco. He commented that General Franco never saw any foreigners alone, but that he would recommend to Franco that he do so in this case.

At one-thirty that afternoon I saw Carrero Blanco again at his office. He told me that I would be received by General Franco at El Pardo at 5 pm that afternoon. I asked the admiral if he would send a car for me, as I did not wish to use an Embassy car with its high-profile diplomatic license plate. He agreed to send a Spanish government car to take me to the *caudillo*. At four-fifteen a car came for me and I drove to General Franco's residence just outside Madrid. As I was well ahead of schedule, I had the driver pull off to the side of the road near the palace and waited to see who went by. López Bravo did and I presumed that he would be present at the interview with Franco. I was thus prepared for this contingency. Carrero Blanco had warned me that Franco was quite old and sometimes seemed feeble. Spaniards did not like him to see foreigners alone. He would try and arrange for me to see Franco alone, but if that were not possible, he hoped that I would understand. Fifteen minutes before my appointment I arrived at El Pardo. I was ushered by liveried footmen into a large waiting room on the second floor of the palace. The walls of this room were entirely covered with yellow silk. The silence of my wait was broken only by the clearly audible ticking of five clocks. Like Adenauer, another old man, Franco was fascinated with time. Spain's great King Emperor Charles V had died in a monastery at Yuste surrounded by clocks.

It was a lonely wait, but not a long one. At exactly five o'clock, I was ushered into Franco's private office. It was the same room where I had seen him once with Eisenhower and twice with Nixon. At his side stood the smiling Foreign Minister. General Franco was in civilian clothes and no one else was present. It was clear to me at this point that to insist on seeing him alone would have been a humiliating affront to the Foreign Minister and I decided not to do this. I opened by thanking General Franco for receiving me and held out the President's letter. He reached out for it but his hand trembled violently and he motioned for the Foreign Minister to take it. López Bravo took the letter and took out of the envelope the

Spanish translation of Mr. Nixon's letter and read it to General Franco, who nodded and asked me to sit down. I then said that I brought greetings from President Nixon, who would never forget the extraordinarily moving welcome he had received in October 1970 from the generalissimo and the Spanish people. I recalled that on arriving at the Moncloa guest palace, the President had said to me: «These people are really our friends». General Franco nodded and said that this was indeed true. I then said that General Franco must know what tremendous burdens the President had to bear; not only did he manage the affairs of the United States but he also bore great world responsibilities. The President greatly valued General Franco's views on the future stability of Spain and the situation of its neighbors.

General Franco spoke first of all of the situation in the Middle East and felt that the death of Nasser had lessened the chances for a settlement in that part of the world. He said that in dealing with the Russians in the SALT talks whatever the Russians signed they would not respect. It was very difficult to get the better of them. I commented with a smile that he had. For an instant, a smile lit the old man's face and he nodded at the compliment. He then said that he felt that what the President was most interested in was what would happen in Spain after his own demise. I replied: «That is correct, General». He said that the succession would be orderly. There was no alternative to the Prince. Spain would move some distance along the road we favored but not all the way, as Spain was neither America nor England nor France. It was Spain. He indicated that the Armed Forces would never let things get out of hand, and expressed confidence in the Prince's ability to handle the situation after his death. He said that he had created a number of institutions to ensure an orderly succession. He smiled and said that many people doubted that these institutions would work. They were wrong; the transition would be peaceful. General Franco then stood up as though to indicate that the interview was over. He said to me: «Tell President Nixon that insofar as the order and stability of Spain are concerned, this will be guaranteed by the timely and orderly measures I am taking». He then asked me to convey to the President his warmest greetings and his gratitude for Mr. Nixon's kind words about the Prince, himself and Spain. We could await the future with full confidence in Spain. He had faith in God and the Spanish people.

I walked slowly downstairs wondering how many men in any walk of life could talk so dispassionately about their own death. I did not believe that this could be very far off. General Franco looked old and weak. His left hand trembled at times so violently that he would cover it with his other hand. At times he appeared far away and at others he came right to the point, as in the remark about his own death and the future stability of Spain. I felt more forgiving toward Lopez Bravo for having worked himself into the interview. If Franco had been my chief of state I would not have wanted to leave him alone with a foreigner. As I drove back for Madrid, I could not but think that Franco had ruled Spain for more than thirty-five years. One way or the other he had given the country peace and a considerable degree of prosperity. Would these be sufficient to guarantee an orderly succession and change of regime? I felt that the President had given me a mission that really required me to do more than talk to General Franco. Ostensibly on leave in Spain, I saw a number of friends in the Spanish Armed Forces who were occupying key positions in the command structure. All of these made quite clear their support for the accession of Prince Juan Carlos on Franco's death and expressed their belief that there would be no disorder or political breakdown in the nation.

All of the senior officers to whom I talked doubted that Franco would place the Prince on the throne before his own death. They did, however, believe that he would appoint a Prime Minister. They did not believe that there would be any disturbances of consequence in the country when Franco died and said that the Armed Forces could easily handle such problems. It was a sobering and unique experience.

I flew back to Washington and there dictated a report to the President in his office. I also spoke to him personally and gave him my impression that the succession would go off in an orderly fashion when the time came. I expressed to him my amazement at the calm and unemotional way in which Franco had discussed the subject. Few men could.

Thus ended my mission to General Franco to discuss the events that would follow his demise. It was a mission unlike any other.

* * *

Two year later I went to Moscow to take part in an International Meeting on Magnetism. Moscow's mayor gave a big reception to the three thousand participants from all over the world. During the reception, a Russian colleague told me a joke about how much the Russians do like vodka and cucumbers, and I felt obliged to correspond with another:

An American and a Russian began a discussion about their respective political systems and the American told the Russian: «In my country everybody can go to the White House and tell the President: President Nixon, you are an idiot! And nothing happens». Then, the Russian told the American: «Well, the same thing in my country, everybody can go to the Kremlin and say: Comrade Brezhnev, President Nixon is an idiot. And nothing happens».

When I was finishing, I noticed a numerous group of colleagues from various nationalities listening attentively. Fortunately, nothing happened.

ADIÓS, FRANCISCO FRANCO, 1975

Frederick D. Wilhelmsen (1923-1996) was a distinguished American scholar, Professor Emeritus of Philosophy and Politics at the University of Dallas, who defined himself as a *citizen of Rome*. He was politically and culturally a Catholic Traditionalist. In the Spanish Civil War, his sympathies were with those *requetés*, who, wearing their red berets, rushed to the Plaza del Castillo in Pamplona for God and country ready to take orders from General Mola on 18th July 1936.

The following is an excerpt from an exceptionally lucid chapter of his book *Citizen of Rome: Reflections from the Life of a Roman Catholic* (1979). His own words are more eloquent than any commentary.

The Valley of the Fallen where Franco is now buried in that huge monastery of granite suggests a peace come to those who have labored in battle. The massive angels who guard the long corridor of the monastery church carved out of the mountain rest on great swords, their eyes closed and their heads bowed as if in sleep. Not the Resurrection but the calm of Holy Saturday after the agony of the Cross permeates that place where veterans of both sides repose now in peace, their war fought –and won or lost–. Franco insisted, against opposition from his own comrades, that families whose sons died fighting for the Red Republic be permitted, should they desire, to have their dead buried with their fallen Catholic foe. It was a gesture of reconciliation and it is to be hoped that all of them now rest in the Lord. But Spain's victory under Franco on this earth was by no means decisive and that victory could be frittered away tomorrow despite the almost forty years Franco had to consolidate his grip on the nation. I can see as in a nightmare the Valley of the Fallen itself dynamited into rubble by a vengeful Red Republic tomorrow...

And thus an assessment of the legacy Franco left his chosen heir Don Juan Carlos de Borbón, is demanded in any eulogy to the memory of the *Caudillo*. After all, Franco warned Spain in his last message pecked out on a typewriter a few days before he went into his final coma that her enemies were alert and again at the door. Nothing is ever forgotten in Spain and no victories are decisive and no defeats are definitive.

Earlier, in the massive demonstration of support Franco received when Europe went wild with hysteria because Spain had executed five terrorists guilty of murdering three times as many policemen, Franco named Spain's enemies from the balcony of the Royal Palace in Madrid: world Masonry and world Communism. The anti-Masonic rhetoric, delivered in his feeble and high pitched voice, was drowned out by the thundering applause of hundreds of thousands of Spaniards who had rallied to their chief because they sensed themselves threatened once again from without and alone. But the rhetoric sounded curiously outdated in this age of ecumenism, and it must have struck most Spaniards that way as they later pondered the meaning of that short five-minute speech. *Masonry* for Franco and for others who had lived through the years of blockade and isolation was a kind of code word, a shorthand, for the entire liberal network of financial and political interests that make up what might be called the *Establishment* of the Western world. And that Establishment is profoundly anti-Catholic and therefore anti-Spanish. That Establishment wants the disestablishment of the Church in Spain as the publicly declared religion of the land. That Establishment today is buttressed by the support of half of the Church in Spain and of well over half of the Church outside Spain. Church and State unity is redolent of the baroque sixteenth century and the Armada and the Inquisition and the whole bag of horrors that form the Black Legend. There hangs about the head of Spain the same halo of hatred, as Chesterton put it, that hangs about the Church of God. The Establishment will not rest until Spain reintroduces the same system of parties that brought it to the brink of ruin in the nineteenth and early twentieth centuries. The Establishment simply does not know or does not care to know that every Spaniard is his own party and his own king and the kind of mechanical discipline needed to make the system work does not exist in Spain. Franco's legacy will receive little comfort and no support at all from the Western democracies, even though a Communist Spain on their Southern flank would mean the end of Europe and the total isolation of the Americas in a world turned into a Red sea. France and everything to its North and East could not survive a Communist Spain. Spanish Communists –and they are numerous and ready to move– are, after all, Spaniards: a favorite sport in Barcelona during the Civil War consisted in mounting machineguns in the portals of churches and spraying the Tabernacle of the Altar. Disinterring dead nuns and violating them publicly ran a close second. Communist or Catholic –Spain is absolutist in its convictions–. If Spain turns from God, the forces of Anti-God will have gained their best ally in Europe. But these considerations do not disturb the Establishment whose unarticulated motto is «Better Red than Roman».

The Communist Party dominates the outlawed Democratic Front which headquarters out of Paris. Basque separatism is more virulent than effective politically. The movement is the result of the Madrid government's stupid policy of not recognizing ancient Basque claims to a measure of autonomy and self-government. This sentiment as incarnated in Carlism is wedded to Spanish unity. When divorced from Carlism, as it has been in large measure in recent times, the cry for Basque autonomy is converted into a cry for independence. The dream of uniting the Five Spanish Basque provinces with the four that lie in France into one nation is a Utopia that Communist tactics have swept into a larger strategy for the dismantling and destroying of Spain as a viable national unit. But neither the Basques nor the Communists have done well by their cause in shooting innocent policemen guarding banks or directing traffic. This kind of public offense to the Spanish Thing is what unites Spaniards who always react to the danger that they can see and never react to the danger that they simply read about.

But the majority of those Spaniards who want a measure of *liberalization* are not Communists or even Socialists. They are Christian Democrats or liberals in the classical political sense of the term and their tradition in Spain dates back to the early nineteenth century. The very word *liberal* is of Hispanic origin and was first used at the Cortes of Cadiz in the post-Napoleonic period under the reign of Ferdinand VII. In a sense Spanish liberalism forms part of the financial and commercial network that knits the Spanish aristocracy into a brotherhood all its own. These people are neither Falangists nor Carlists. They desire a ceremonial monarchy under a king who exercises some influence but little power and their political vision extends no further than 1931 when the old system collapsed and the king fled the country. For this influential class, Franco has been little more than an interlude and the horrors of the Communist Republic have been dimmed in memory thanks to the passing of time. Given that Juan Carlos's very title to the crown reaches back to the dominant liberalism of the last century, he is bound by the pressure of history to yield, if but partially and possibly reluctantly, to a class that always despised Franco even as it waxed economically on the peace he secured Spain.

King Juan Carlos finds himself in a typical double, even triple, bind: damned if he does and damned if he doesn't. The Falangists and other right-wing elements, including the police and most of the army, want to hold the line against dismantling Franco's Spain. Their most eloquent leader today is the lay theologian, Blas Piñar. The most savagely right-wing force today is the police: too many of their own are being picked off by Communists and separatists who announced in March a policy of killing one policeman a day until the government surrendered to their demands. They are batting about 300 percent and that is good hitting in any man's league. Juan Carlos is already being pressured by the Right to resist any significant move towards change. The classical liberals of wealth, prestige, and title will expect the king to repudiate Franco and return to the old days of Alfonso XIII. They would have preferred Don Juan, but they can live with his son provided that he do their will. The powerful *Opus Dei* which cuts through all non-Communist political divisions will want some liberalization but not too much. The Church is split and polarized into Right and Left, the former being captained by the Cardinal Primate of Toledo and the latter by the Cardinal of Madrid. Premier Arias Navarro, who broke down over national television when he read Franco's *adiós* to Spain, is too soft for the Right, especially the police, and he is too hard for the proponents of liberalization. At this writing he has not offered his resignation to the new king, but he is not required to do so by law. He could, of course, be fired or kept on at the sovereign's will. The post-Franco constitution is sufficiently open-ended that Juan Carlos can make of it what he wants: he can both reign and govern or he can let his ministers govern and retire discreetly into the background and assume the *English* role that the liberals have painted for him –a monarchy of plenty of pomp and circumstance but little substance–. Such a monarchy cannot last for long in these declining years of the twentieth century. Much depends on the character of Juan Carlos and very little is known of his worth, except that he is a gentleman and the husband of a fiercely ambitious woman, Sophia of Greece, who inherited her passion for power from her mother. Juan Carlos has been taught some traditionalist history and doctrine by his former tutor, Fr. Federico Suárez of the *Opus Dei,* Spain's leading historian of the nineteenth century and a man whose youth was spent in the Carlist movement whose discipline he subsequently abandoned but whose ideas he has retained. In any event, Juan Carlos has been catapulted to power –or political oblivion–, but nobody was ever prepared more carefully for kingship than was the prince by General Franco.

And thus Francisco Franco died at the very moment when his ancient enemies began to strike again. This man never thought of himself as a dictator. He left an elaborate constitution which gives representation in the Cortes to the heads of families and to professions and guilds. Individual members of the Cortes defied Franco from time to time on the floor before their peers and their right to do so was never denied nor were they harassed in their private lives. Franco lived by the rules he established, but his personality was such that whatever he willed became law. Those days are now dead and with them have gone the security and peace of an age.

Spain will hold the line for Christian civilization if the men in power keep their nerve. If they yield under foreign pressure, then Spain will slide inevitably to the Left and ultimately to Communism. The victory of Francisco Franco was only an interlude and a holding action in a war as ancient as history itself. And now the old warrior has been buried deep behind the main altar of the basilica of the Valley of the Fallen. A hundred thousand comrades, veterans of the war mingling with young Rightists, sang the Falangist *Cara al Sol* and cried out as one man «Long live Franco». But he is dead, and only one lonely voice exclaimed «Long live the King» as Juan Carlos, pensive and grim of visage, watched the coffin of his mentor disappear under the mountain.

* * *

Everybody in Spain knew that Franco's authoritarian system could not last for ever. But, was Franco right when he chose Don Juan Carlos as his heir and solicited for him the loyalty and unconditional support of all those who had been his followers?

That is the question.

Franco, in all likelihood, might have arranged things in such a way that the future king were, from the beginning, a purely decorative figure. This is what he became from 1978 on, after the ambivalent Constitution was voted into the law of the country. Martín Villa (a former Falangist, turned into *progressive* social-democrat), the UCD minister, informed the Spaniards about the Referendum outcome on television. He was not very convincing.

Alternatively, the way could have been left open to a more flexible and more truly representative transition, a transition which could have ended in a true Traditional Catholic Monarchy or in a Constitutional Presidential Republic. (Most middle-aged and young people in Spain were *not* Monarchist at the time, and *not* Republican either).

Now, almost forty years after Franco's death, it is abundantly clear that the so called democratic transition was not done well. The King, his mentors and his close collaborators left then the extreme left (the Communist Party, CCOO, the Basque and Catalan separatists...) to take the initiative, financed and comfortably seconded by the establishment and the banks.

Definitely, it would have been preferable for the country either to have a decorative King from the beginning or a Constitutional Presidential Republic with proper checks and balances also from the very beginning.

If Franco's good health had lasted only four or five years more, he might have seen a Polish Roman Pontiff restoring some health to the Catholic Church; and an American President setting into motion events which would dynamite for good the Soviet empire.

But, of course, no victories are for ever in this world. And no defeats.

EPILOGUE

The Spanish Civil War was *not* a conflict in which terrible wrongdoing by both sides can be distributed symmetrically. The wrongdoings of the Popular Front were incomparably more in number and more outrageous.

After the victory of the Nationalists in 1939, the repression was understandable, given the circumstances. Just think in what the repression would have been in the case of a victory of the Popular Front: If one takes seriously typical statements by *Pasionaria*, Largo Caballero and Durruti, the victims after the war would have been easily two million or more, judging by the inhuman hatred shown by socialists, communists and anarchists during the first three months of the war. Not generally known, it may be noted that even the separatists had *checas* in Madrid, Bilbao and Barcelona.

So the repression of Franco's government was understandable given the terrible circumstances. There were exceptions, special cases of cruelty in the Nationalist half Spain, but, of course, those exceptions do confirm the general rule. It may be noted also that Carlist leaders protested early those excesses.

In summary:

The Spanish Civil War was *not* a romantic war of secession in which Basque and Catalan separatists were fighting against an oppressive centralist government: the oppression was nonexistent.

It was *not* a conflict of democracy and freedom against totalitarian oppression, as leftist propaganda pretended then and now. The Popular Front was specially in the first months a paradigm of totalitarian oppression mixed with anarchy.

The Spanish Civil War was above all a war of religion: the Christian Catholic way of life against the Marxist-Leninist and Anarchist way of life.

A good recent reminder of this undeniable fact was the beatification of 522 Spanish martyrs, mostly from Catalonia, on 13th October 2013.

INDEX

United Nations, 149
United States, 5, 121, 170, 177
Universidad Complutense, 141
Universidad Complutense
   (Madrid), 67
University of Caen, 93
University of Dallas, 180
USA, 70
Utopia, 24, 182

V

Valdes, J., 75
Valencia, 24, 28, 45, 49, 64, 68,
   77, 91, 92, 93, 94, 125, 136
Valladolid, 62, 63, 64, 129
Valley of the Fallen, 42, 180, 184
Varela, Captain, 30
Varela, General, 35, 36, 130, 131,
   132, 133, 134
Vatican, 43
Vegas Perez, Captain, 44
Ventaja, Bishop of Almeria, 47
Vichy Government, 117
Vidal i Barraquer, Cardinal, 68, 69
Vidal, C., 68, 69, 76, 127
Vienna, 62
Villa Abrille, General, 66
Villacarrillo, 51
Vitoria, F, de, 37
Viva Cristo Rey, 34, 45, 47

Viva España, 29, 32, 41, 47, 152
Viva la muerte, 39
Viva Rusia, 41

W

Walters, V., 7, 170, 174, 175
War of Independence, 146
War of Reconquest, 30
War of the Galaxies, 168
Washington, G., 165, 167, 178
We will overcome, 160
Wilhelmsen, F. D., 180
World, 147, 149
Wyszynski, Cardinal, 8

Y

Yagüe, General, 24, 30, 130, 131,
   132, 133, 134, 135
Yagüe, J., 24, 30, 130, 131, 132,
   133, 134, 135
Yalta, 152
Yo Escogí la Esclavitud, 120

Z

Zamora, 26, 115, 116
Zaragoza, 24
Zocodover, Plaza, 26, 27, 28, 34
Zubiri, J., 84

Printed in Great Britain
by Amazon.co.uk, Ltd.,
Marston Gate.